W9-BEH-215

exploring REIKI

108 Questions and Answers

DR. LAXMI PAULA HORAN

author of
Empowerment Through Reiki

New Page Books
A division of The Career Press, Inc.
Franklin Lakes, NJ

Copyright © 2005 by Dr. Laxmi Paula Horan

All rights reserved under the Pan-American and International Copyright Conventions. This book may not be reproduced, in whole or in part, in any form or by any means electronic or mechanical, including photocopying, recording, or by any information storage and retrieval system now known or hereafter invented, without written permission from the publisher, The Career Press.

EXPLORING REIKI
EDITED AND TYPESET BY CLAYTON W. LEADBETTER
Cover photo: K. Vey, JumpFoto
Cover design by Design Concepts
Printed in the U.S.A. by Book-mart Press

Photos courtesy of Keku Writer, Bombay
Model, Katharine Rupert

To order this title, please call toll-free 1-800-CAREER-1 (NJ and Canada: 201-848-0310) to order using VISA or MasterCard, or for further information on books from Career Press.

The Career Press, Inc., 3 Tice Road, PO Box 687,
Franklin Lakes, NJ 07417
www.careerpress.com
www.newpagebooks.com

Library of Congress Cataloging-in-Publication Data

Horan, Laxmi.
    Exploring reiki : 108 questions and answers / by Laxmi Paula Horan.
       p. cm.
    Includes index.
    ISBN 1-56414-823-8 (pbk.)
    1. Reiki (Healing system) I. Title.

RZ403.R45H668 2005
616.8′52--dc22

                                       2005041539

*Dedicated to my students worldwide,
who have acted as much as my teachers
as I have acted as theirs.*

ACKNOWLEDGMENTS

Thank you, Papaji, for the gift of boundless love and life, without separation.

Thank you, Kate, for introducing me to mastership.

Thank you, all of my students in the four corners of the world, for sharing the incredible presence of Universal Life Force Energy with me.

Thank you, Narayan, for your shoulder to lean on and your knowledge, love, and wisdom which I constantly draw on.

Thank you, Shekhar and Poonam for friendship and encouragment.

Thank you, universe, for your innumerable acts of generosity and synchronicity.

CONTENTS

Chapter 5: Second Degree Basics 107

Chapter 6: Third Degree Basics 121

PREFACE

Similar to my first book, *Empowerment Through Reiki*, this volume is written in appreciation of the ease and down-to-earth directness with which the Usui Method of Natural Healing can be practiced—and its manifold benefits enjoyed. Reiki's absolute simplicity is it's greatest asset. When we stick to the basics, over time, Reiki very naturally gifts us with the undiluted experience of its effectiveness and subtlety. We feel its soothing and balancing influences in our lives and in the midst of the challenges that we encounter every day. Likewise, we are able to convey these benefits to others. On the basis of this experience, the good message can be heard and spread that, indeed, everyone's body/mind contains this incredible and unfathomable self-healing power, which can be accessed to our own and our environment's advantage.

In response to past published works, I have received many letters and communications from Reiki masters and practitioners who express their gratitude for highly readable guidance in putting Reiki into practice so that its original intention of simple hands-on healing and self-healing can be adapted to almost any situation. It is my sincere wish that this book should be as helpful.

Over the last decade, many titles have been published on the subject of Reiki, including two more of my own, *Abundance Through Reiki* and *The Ultimate Reiki Touch*.

However, among all of the books on Reiki, this succinct introduction into the practice is unique in the sense that it directly addresses the main questions that are asked time and again by students in all of the countries where I have taught. In this regard, the book can easily address the various doubts that can arise regarding the subtleties of Reiki practice when we venture out on our own. The answers aim to point the reader toward a greater understanding of the essence of this ungraspable and indefinable Universal Life Force Energy for the purpose of healing and bringing more balance into our lives.

The point of the questions and answers, therefore, is not so much to tell you what you should think and take as unquestionable truth about any particular aspect of the Usui System; rather, they are intended to guide you in deepening your practice and, on the basis of your own experience, help you feel and think for yourself. It is the book's purpose to act as a mirror for you. In it, you will find your own answers, which evolve with continuous careful and deliberate experimentation with Reiki. As you continue to feel and think for yourself in another area of your life, all other areas are also affected. Thus the process of liberation and emancipation from long held limiting beliefs will naturally progress, and through your individual existence, you inevitably will touch and change anything that limits the original goodness inherent in all of creation. This is a profound healing experience.

Laxmi Paula Horan
Full Moon Day, December 2004

INTRODUCTION

Have you ever noticed how, occasionally in life, when you plan a new project and begin focusing your energies to get it off the ground, something else that still needs to be completed inevitably draws your attention before you can move on to your new project? When you then take up the challenge and follow what is spontaneously arising, you actually clear the way for what you wanted to do in the first place. This is exactly, how *Exploring Reiki: 108 Questions and Answers* came about.

Originally, I had planned to write another book at this time, called *True Reiki True Self*. I had even completed the first few chapters, when I had to interrupt the process to go on yet another long extended teaching tour. *True Reiki True Self*, as I envisioned it, would become an inspiring testimony in poetic language to the unfathomable healing essence of Universal Life Force Energy. Drawing on my own experience and sharing many of my own stories, I wanted to give the reader a taste of how truly limitless Reiki can be. At least, that was my plan, which will now come to fruition much later than anticipated.

During my tour, I was asked to write a book with the bare essentials of Reiki, in order to clarify some widespread misunderstandings. Initially, I resisted this project of a "back to basics" Reiki book. Having previously authored three books on Reiki, *Empowerment Through*

Reiki (1990), *Abundance Through Reiki* (1995), and *The Ultimate Reiki Touch* (2002), I felt I had already fully covered the basics. What my associates and my husband so aptly pointed out is how profoundly my teaching has changed over the years. It has become simpler and more straightforward. Perhaps I could convey this to a larger audience.

After getting over my initial resistance, this book developed its own flow and simply happened. It truly wrote itself, and I derived a lot of pleasure from participating in its creation. The result is a joyful dialogue on the utter beauty, the utter simplicity, that is Reiki.

There has been an amazing array of information put out on Reiki in the last few years. Although several good books have been written by a few of the more mature practitioners, the sheer volume of the information now available is sometimes confusing and contradictory to the reader and is often even totally unrelated to Reiki. Typically, procedures from other healing methods are added to Reiki, which adds to the confusion.

For most people in the early stages of Reiki practice, it is hard to grasp just how simple Reiki is. There is a tendency for the beginning practitioner's (and the beginning teacher's) mind to try to make it more complex. The mind (ego) seems to need a lot of unnecessary rules, regulations, and accoutrements to convince itself that something as simple as Reiki actually works without added on "doodads," even though his or her hands palpably tell him or her just the opposite!

In this book, I hope to help a broader public by dispelling a lot of the disinformation that I have been confronted with in my own Reiki classes and that I have heard all too often from other teachers in recent years. Most important, my intention is to explore the basic facets in a clear and simple manner, from my viewpoint, after 16 years of experience both practicing and teaching Reiki in several different countries.

The information has been kept short and to the point. However, oversimplification has also been carefully avoided. The intention is to present something similar to a reference work, yet in an easy, user-friendly format. The idea is to provide you with something like a companion or guide that can address the queries which inevitably surface.

When formulating the questions, I was able to draw on the many classes that I have taught since 1987. I purposely chose the questions that my students most often ask me during or directly after a Reiki class.

Teaching happens in a natural flow when it takes the form of a dialogue. The question and answer format seemed appropriate to recreate the sense of engaging in a dialogue with the reader. The philosophers of ancient Greece did not hold professorships. They went about Athens and talked to just about everyone. Likewise, the Buddha didn't sit under a tree to scribble scriptures on palm leaves. Instead, he wandered all over Northern India and engaged people in conversations whenever they were interested in listening to what he had to share.

When I teach a class, people ask me questions and I respond spontaneously to whatever is invoked by the questioner. This is precisely the feeling I tried to achieve in this book—the feeling of a live dialogue between student and teacher. Here, many of the topics are dealt with that regularly come up during a Reiki class. You could say the book is the next best thing to taking a class with me. The only drawback is that I am not personally present to clarify points or dispel doubts. However, if you use this book as intended, you will find that a careful examination of the pertinent passages will eventually give you the answers that you were looking for, which are actually already inside of you. In order to ask a question, you already have to have intuitively grasped a large part of the answer. Answers are really just to dispel doubts. Whenever you are in doubt or feel that a certain question about the basic practice of Reiki has been left unanswered, go back and look up the relevant sections of the text.

Let's face it. Humans are forgetful. Even if you pay close attention, you are bound to disregard a lot of things that were mentioned in your Reiki class. Furthermore, studies have shown that even good students, on the average, absorb only 35 percent of the information given to them at any one time—which explains why you have to go back and study the things you really want to learn. Because the human mind generally doesn't have the capacity to absorb all of the information it receives, it helps to have a reliable source you can go back to whenever you need clarification.

This book fulfills yet another need. Considering that usually only 35 percent of the information given at any one time is retained, what do you think will happen to basic Reiki knowledge, which can only be integrated experientially, if passed on through a line of teachers who became Reiki masters within a week or a month, and then proceeded to initiate others into mastership shortly thereafter? How much accurate knowledge will remain after three or four generations of teachers and students of this kind? Under such conditions, a book of basic Reiki questions and answers can be of great assistance for those who want to go back to its real roots.

Overall, I have kept the book within the boundaries of Reiki, as taught by Hawayo Takata. At present, most Reiki practitioners can trace their lineage back to Dr. Usui and the Usui Method of Natural Healing (*Usui Shiki Ryoho*) through Mrs. Takata and one of her 22 master students who made Reiki popular all around the world. Therefore, particular emphasis has been put on her form of Reiki, simply because it is the most widely practiced and, yet, often the most misunderstood—even to the point of complete distortion. *Exploring Reiki: 108 Questions and Answers* is my own contribution to help clear some of the most common misunderstandings in a gentle and nonjudgmental manner.

That there are altogether 108 questions and answers listed in this book is, of course, no mere coincidence. The total of the digits in 108 is 9. In turn, 9 is the only number which, when multiplied by any integer, reproduces itself (or a multiple of itself) as the sum of the digits. For example: $3 \times 9 = 27$ and $2 + 7 = 9$, or $4 \times 9 = 36$ and $3 + 6 = 9$, and so forth. Therefore, 9 is seen as the number of completion. As the product of 9×12, 108 is regarded as a particularly auspicious number, which is why it was chosen for this book: to convey the auspicious presence of Universal Life Force Energy.

For further information, in Appendix A, I have included an essay on the full body treatment, its effect on the endocrine system, the endocrine system's connection to the immune system, and its role in healing, because this is where Mrs. Takata focused her attention in her own treatments, besides treating the major organs of the body.

In most other books on Reiki, references to the endocrine system remain scanty. Instead, their focus is on more esoteric and etheric levels of organization. For this basic presentation of the principles of hands-on and distant healing with Universal Life Force Energy, I have refrained from getting too esoteric. In this instance, it did indeed seem counterproductive.

In a second essay, in Appendix B, I have discussed at length why Reiki may prove particularly helpful in this day and age, as each individual's very own personal declaration of independence from drugs and unnecessary outside interventions.

Through the actual practice of Reiki, all of the answers you will ever need will come to you as if by osmosis. It is important to remember that all *in*formation comes from the outside and is ultimately mind-stuff. Therefore, it is essential not to get stuck in or attached to any of the answers contained in the text. It is better to let the answers instead act as an inspiration to help you create your own response—to help you get in touch with your own inner knowing.

Practicing Reiki supports you in tapping your own feelings. All of *your* answers lie within the superior intelligence of your heart. Thus, the ability to feel, which Reiki promotes due to its very essence as heart energy, will help you to find your own answers. For those who need support in letting go of resistance to feelings, this book may provide insights to assist you further along the path.

Ultimately, the proof "in the pudding," regarding Reiki, is in the practice. I wish you much comfort, ease, and joy in your work with Reiki. Share it with yourself and others as often as possible, because the more you call on Universal Life Force Energy the sooner it will respond.

Chapter 1

BASIC REIKI

*T*his first group of entries concerns the Reiki basics, with questions and answers that deal with the qualities that define Reiki. They provide the background information we need to be aware of, if we wish to practice the Usui Method of Natural Healing. They also describe the framework of deeply spiritual and compassionate values, which were intended by its founder and the age-old lineage of natural and spiritual healers who served as his source of inspiration. History, structure, method of transmission—this chapter addresses all of these and helps you to understand and grasp the true and liberating spirit of Reiki.

1. What is Reiki?

Most commonly, the word *Reiki* refers to a simple hands-on healing technique, a form of energy medicine, rediscovered by Dr. Mikao Usui in Japan in the late 19th century. Dr. Usui chose the term *Reiki* to describe

Universal Life Force Energy, which calms the mind and raises a person's life force. Through the use of soothing hands laid on the body in certain positions, the process of healing is accelerated. The essence of this form of healing, in Reiki, is passed on from teacher to student through a series of mystic initiations that, like in the Tantric forms of Buddhism in Japan or Tibet, are called *attunements* or *empowerments.*

In actuality, Reiki is the fundamental nature or substratum of the universe, and the Usui Method of Natural Healing is an easy way of giving back to yourself more of what you already fundamentally are: Universal Life Force Energy. You literally recharge yourself with that which, at the deepest level, you have always been.

In quantum physics, as well as hermetic science, energy is recognized as the fundamental nature of existence. In truth, there is no solid matter. Thus, the human body, thoughts, and emotions are all composed of energy oscillating at various frequencies. The denser the vibration, the more apt we are to experience discomfort or "dis-ease." The freer the vibration, the greater the chance for natural health, abundance, beauty, satisfaction, and well-being.

Through getting the body/mind in touch with Universal Life Force Energy, its very own substratum, Reiki can release the individual in a gentle and gradual manner from age-old restrictions and bondage and allow him or her, over time, to first experience vibrant health and balance and, finally, experience freedom and unity.

2. Where does Reiki come from?

In its outer appearance as energy medicine, Reiki very likely has its real roots in India, having passed through Tibet and China to Japan, where it was rediscovered by

Dr. Usui. In its unlimited inner potential, Reiki comes from nowhere in particular, because it is everywhere and exists as everything. In this aspect of Universal Life Force Energy, Reiki is unknowable and ungraspable, and yet can be directly experienced by everyone at every moment due to its all-pervasive nature.

In a deeper sense, as Universal Life Force Energy itself, Reiki is the substratum or underlying nature of everything. It exists everywhere. Because of our identification with the body and its five senses, we have forgotten that, in actuality, we are the very unlimitedness of being itself. We don't recall the powers granted to us; by simply being open and aware, we can draw whatever resources we need directly to us (much like Christ manifesting the fish and the loaves or a present-day realized master accomplishing things that go beyond our normal understanding).

Through the attunements or empowerments of Reiki (which reestablish the direct energetic channel we have for Universal Life Force Energy to flow through), we begin to reconnect (or simply notice) the direct link we've always had with all the energy there is. We begin to draw in directly what we need from what at first seems to come from the outside. Then we slowly regain the knowledge that all we are *is* within the all-inclusive mystical Heart of hearts (including our bodies), although the mind cannot possibly comprehend the oneness of all of reality.

3. How does Reiki heal?

By calming the mind and raising the life force energy in the body.

The body is actually energy vibrating at a certain frequency, and all its frequencies have their own natural flow. However, when we make a judgment about something (rather than discernment), the judgment gets stored in the cellular structure of the body in the form of a physical and/or emotional block. Emotions are a reaction to our thoughts or judgments about people and life's situations. Because they distort the natural frequencies, negative thoughts or judgments are experienced as dense or uncomfortable vibrations. Such thoughts may turn into headaches, tension, stomach aches, or ulcers. Rage and anger or grief held in the body can easily turn into tumors. In the same way, mental control "trips" or the power trips we bought into from others can turn into rheumatoid arthritis.

Provided we stick to the tried and proven procedures outlined by any good, traditional Reiki teacher, Reiki, over time, may actually heal all of these blockages. Reiki exposes them to the much higher vibratory frequency of Universal Life Force Energy, which can then penetrate and dissolve any block.

By simple laying on of hands over the entire body so that it can draw the energy it needs, Reiki helps us to feel our feelings fully, so they can easily pass through the body/mind and not get stuck. Old stuck thoughts (through treatment) have their frequencies raised and then are enabled to also pass through.

Thus Reiki heals by raising our life force frequency.

4. Who is Dr. Mikao Usui?

Dr. Mikao Usui is the founder of the modern-day Reiki movement. According to recently found information, he was a Tendai Buddhist practitioner, family man, and healer. Born in 1865 into a family of minor aristocracy, as a young man he was originally encouraged to go into business; but this was not his true proclivity, so he instead studied the Japanese and Chinese healing arts, and later

Western allopathic medicine with Christian missionary doctors.

Due to a powerful spiritual experience on sacred Mount Kurama, which he later described to several of his students, he gained a tremendous natural ability to heal through the laying on of hands. Through contemplation and further meditative experiences he then discovered how to pass his abilities on to others.

He coined the term *Reiki* (Universal Life Force Energy), as it conveys how healing with Reiki is accomplished by allowing soothing healing energies to simply flow through the palms of your hands.

Dr. Usui passed away in 1926. As he predicted during the last years of his life, his legacy did indeed survive and is now benefiting people everywhere. If we recognize him as the true healer and dedicated humanitarian that he was and emulate his example, we will infuse our own Reiki practice with the devotion and dedication that it deserves. Dr. Usui literally showed us a way to connect with Universal Life Force Energy, the source of all healing.

5. How is Reiki different from other healing methods?

Reiki is a form of energy medicine similar to Touch for Health or Pranic Healing. The essential difference is Reiki's utter simplicity (besides a few hand positions, there is no methodology to learn) and the recognition that no one ever heals anyone else—that all healing is pure Grace and just *happens*.

For example, if I lay my hands on you to "do" a treatment, your body will simply draw what it needs through the channel. You can actually be doubtful or skeptical, because Reiki ultimately transcends the mind; however, you do need to be at least open to the possibility of receiving

Reiki. Your body will then of its own innate intelligence simply draw in what it needs.

Thus, in Reiki, I don't have to sit there and try to make the energy flow. Simply by my intention to share a treatment, the energy begins to be *drawn* into the other, and this is the key: Reiki is always drawn, never sent, even at the Second Degree level, when distant treatments are shared.

One only has to learn how to listen to one's hands. Through the recognition of our true state of "non-doing" (that everything which happens in the universe happens due to pure Grace), Reiki could be aptly called the simplest of all healing arts.

6. Is there more than one form of authentic Reiki?

Yes, there are several authentic forms and lineages of Reiki, but not everything that calls itself Reiki actually is Reiki. Among the authentic forms and lineages are the following:

1. Traditional Reiki, as taught through the direct lineage of Usui, Hayashi, Takata, and her 22 direct students (provided that every master further down the line has kept the transmission pure and teaches it in its essential form).

2. All lineages that go back to Dr. Usui through Dr. Hayashi and his student Sensei Takeuchi, a Zen monk who received a different set of teachings from Dr. Hayashi than Mrs. Takata.

3. Usui Reiki Ryoho Gakkei, the traditional Reiki that has been practiced in Japan itself in an unbroken lineage and is not connected to Mrs. Takata.

Because Dr. Usui had a number of close students, there may be other authentic forms and lineages of Reiki that still remain quietly hidden by the wayside.

However, due to the popularity of the Usui Method of Natural Healing and the increasing demand for it around the world, a number of questionable teachers have also appeared. A few people have begun adding so-called "channeled" symbols and attunements and have created new forms and haphazard healing techniques to which they attach the word *Reiki*. I do not wish to mention any of them specifically and prefer to leave that to your own discernment. Usually these mental creations carry as their name a catchy noun or combination of nouns in connection with the word *Reiki*.

The Reiki channel is always inherently there in all sentient beings, so anyone with a certain amount of charisma can also help you feel some form of energy. If you believe in them, it will work up to a certain point. What you will be missing, though, is the connection with the genuine lineage of Reiki as conveyed by Dr. Usui through the vehicle of the attunements.

Very few Reiki masters or teachers practicing today are self-realized. In other words, most Reiki masters are more like masters of a craft but do not possess the qualities usually associated with a *spiritual* master, let alone a fully enlightened being. This means that the seed energy for the opening of the Reiki channel is carried only by the attunements the individual teacher has received from his or her own master. The teacher does not fully embody it at every moment; rather it is carried through him or her and only called upon when needed.

If the Reiki master were a spiritual master in the true sense, he or she would live uninterruptedly in full conscious awareness of Universal Life Force Energy. It would be ever-present, and the feeling of separation and alienation from all of reality, including other sentient beings, would never even arise. However, despite a lack of this quality of all-pervasive awareness the Reiki master can still act as a master and convey attunements.

There are two reasons: First, like any other being or appearance in this universe, the Reiki master is by nature nothing other than the very universal life force energy he or she is empowering or attuning others to. Therefore, in his or her aspect of wholeness, the individual teacher is always realized, even though this realization may go unnoticed. Second, the teacher has learned through practice and experience to quiet the mind when conveying attunements so that he or she can then tap into this aspect of wholeness and inseparability and convey its taste. At other times, when this is not possible, when the teacher is unable to quiet the mind and be fully present and aware during the time of empowerment, the "weight" of the empowerment is carried through the vehicle of the teacher by mere intention and the fact that they have been empowered to do so.

Obviously, the closer a Reiki master is to deeper levels of realization, the better he or she can awaken to awareness of the ever-presence of Universal Life Force Energy in the student who is receiving the empowerment. In other words, full self-realization infers continuous presence of awareness, not being lost in or identified with any thought that is moving through the mindstream. This does not mean that a self-realized being does not have any thoughts, or emotions, or sense perceptions. Thought, emotion, and sense perception may be moving through the mindstream of the individual, but an awareness of their total openness is also present.

Such a state of openness allows the Reiki teacher to act as a pure mirror for what is actually the self-empowerment of the student, so that the Reiki energy, which the Reiki student already exists as, finally becomes apparent to the student. Essentially, the teacher acts as a mirror to help the student become aware of what has always been there, waiting to be noticed. The main role of the teacher is to remove doubt and help the student perceive directly what has always been there right in front of his or her eyes— but what they have been conditioned to ignore.

In this context, a story from Captain Cook's discovery of New Zealand in the 1700s comes to mind. When his ship anchored in a bay, the Maori natives could not even see it because, through their experience to date, they had not been conditioned that such big ships could exist. They could only see the small rowing boats that Captain Cook had sent to shore, because they were about the same size as their own vessels. In a way, due to our conditioning to believe in only what we can see or touch, when it comes to Reiki energy, we are like the Maoris who couldn't see the big ship because they had not been taught to do so. The role of the Reiki master is then to point out the all-pervasive ever-presence of this energy, much like a really big ship in our lives that can carry us to the land of greater freedom, better health, and deeper harmony with all of existence.

As Dr. Usui is the origin of all present-day Reiki lineages, it is thus important to at least find a Reiki master in one of the proper lineages, who can share attunements that go back to Dr. Usui and very possibly an ancient lineage of practitioners.

7. What are attunements?

Attunements (or empowerments) are the essential ingredients in any Reiki class. At the First Degree level, there are four attunements, and at Second and Third Degree, one attunement each.

Reiki attunements are essentially a ritualized ceremony which convey the essence or seed kernel of that which you already are (Universal Life Force Energy), in such a way that the initial veils of ignorance are removed so that you can begin to experience the direct link that you have always had with all the energy there is (because that is what you truly are).

As within any tradition in which empowerments are given, such as in the empowerments given by Tibetan Lamas or Shingon Buddhist masters, it is necessary to find a master teacher within that same tradition who has received and integrated the oral teachings and imbibed the wisdom energetically through practice and through a direct connection with a living master in the tradition. Therefore, Reiki empowerments can be properly given only by a Reiki master/teacher who is in the direct lineage of Dr. Mikao Usui and who has worked with Reiki extensively, preferably over many years.

It is my experience, due to the flood of students seeking to be reattuned, that most of the forms of so-called "Reiki"—with a lot of superfluous added-on names and probably newly invented symbols and abbreviated attunements—carry very little essence behind them. For this reason, it is important to connect with a teacher in one of the direct lineages of Dr. Mikao Usui.

Attunements, on a practical level, raise a person's life force energy and reawaken them to the Reiki channel so that they may treat themselves, and as an added benefit, also treat others. At the First Degree level, much focus is directed toward the physical body so that, at the cellular level, the vibratory rate is amplified. People often experience emotional and physical cleansings as a result, as much density is sloughed off.

At the Second Degree level, the amplification seems to center more on the etheric or energy body, which contains the chakras, or main subtle energy centers. Further emotional and physical cleansings can occur with an accompanying opening at an intuitive level. Because of this opening, which sometimes brings psychic abilities with it, many people become excited, and are then drawn to do Third Degree prematurely.

The focus of Third Degree is actually about dropping your power "trip." The Third Degree attunement, if given too early, seems not to amplify your energy—only your ego, when you are not properly prepared. Thus we see tremendous ignorance today being acted out by many so-called "Reiki masters." Overall, the attunements affect each individual according to their own evolution and never bring out more than you are ready for. The Third Degree attunement is the one attunement that should be postponed as long as is appropriate, in order to gain full benefit.

8. How can I tell if I have chosen a suitable Reiki master?

From the previous question and answer, it should now be obvious why discernment is essential in choosing a Reiki teacher. Ideally, you want to choose a Reiki master who carries both the essence (through a detached yet joyful and openhearted noticing and sharing of the everpresence of Universal Life Force Energy) and can convey the attunements of the Usui Method of Natural Healing.

Some of the key questions you may want to ask a prospective Reiki teacher are:

1. *How long have you practiced Reiki?* (Hopefully at least three years before becoming a master.)

2. *Can you trace your lineage back to Dr. Usui?* (The attunements which are given should be in Dr. Usui's transmission to ensure that you

will receive the essence or seed kernel of Grace which helps to truly unveil the Reiki channel.)

3. *Do you feel at peace in your master's/teacher's presence?* (Although sometimes a true teacher may challenge the status quo—your ego—and temporarily make you feel off balance, overall you should feel a sense of peace in their presence.)

Any other questions which come to mind are pertinent (otherwise they wouldn't come up). Also, notice if they are overly impressed with all the people "they have healed" (Remember, in Reiki, healing just happens!) or maintain a sense of equanimity about themselves and life in general.

A genuine Reiki master will never proselytize Reiki. They most assuredly will be enthusiastic, but especially, should never push people to do Second and Third Degree.

Basically, you want to find a well-balanced person with a positive outlook. University degrees, professional certificates, or logos on letterheads are not as important as basic common sense. The final sign of a good teacher is that, in an overall sense, they challenge you, but at the same time make you feel good about yourself. In other words, they don't aggrandize themselves (their precious ego) at your expense. They don't make you feel small, but rather inspire you to directly experience that you are Universal Life Force itself!

9. Is there such a thing as a "grand master" in Reiki?

No, there isn't. Dr. Usui, who through arduous effort reformulated Reiki and became the founder of the entire modern-day Reiki movement, never even thought of referring to himself as "grand master." If he didn't, why should anyone else? In all spiritual traditions the world over, honorary titles are sometimes bestowed upon those rare individuals who totally live what they teach and are surrounded by an aura of absolute realization. In that sense, Dr. Usui and someone like him actually could be considered a true grand master. The point is that he never called himself such. The bottom line is that whoever finds it necessary to call him- or herself "grand master" is still far removed from true mastership, let alone "grand" mastership.

Another factor that contributed to the creation of literally hundreds of "grand masters" can be found in the improper way Third Degree has been taught by splitting it into "3A" and "3B." A new terminology was created to decipher the difference between the two. In my opinion, there is no such thing as a "half master." You either are or you aren't. Some inexperienced Reiki masters adopted the idea that giving the Third Degree attunements would help others in their spiritual growth and "boost" their power. Some ill-informed people even teach 3A in a class format and give large numbers the Third Degree attunement as a marketing ploy. Those who later decide they want to teach can then pay another fee and learn how to do the attunements and teach. Because students who had only received the Third Degree symbol and attunement (3A) began to call themselves Reiki masters, some of the people who had completed 3B opted for calling themselves "grand masters," in order to stand out.

Nowadays, there are many people calling themselves "grand masters" who don't even have 3A, 3B, or *any* authentic Reiki attunement for that matter. The whole thing has become a joke. A true master (in the sense of having mastered the ego/mind) would never even call himself master, let alone add the title "grand." For myself, I use the title *Reiki master* much in the same way as a master craftsperson would. In other words, no claim is made beyond the ability to share correct Reiki attunements that go back to Dr. Usui.

10. How is Reiki taught?

Reiki is taught in three stages, or Degrees, in order to help the student properly integrate the empowerments, or attunements. (It takes 21 days just for the physical body to process the attunements at each level.) Teaching Reiki in stages also helps the student to gain adequate experience and understanding of the subtlety of Reiki at each level.

First Degree Reiki, comprising four attunements, can be given throughout a four-day period (one attunement per day) or, minimally, a two-day period, as there needs to be at least 24 hours between the second and third attunement. Two full days or four full evenings are required for the First Degree class, in order for the students to properly learn the hand positions and complete enough treatments to gain confidence to work on their own.

First Degree treatments should be practiced a minimum of three months before considering Second Degree. Even a period of six months or longer is a good idea, to reap the full benefit of Second Degree. Second Degree can be taught in only 4 or 5 hours, but I have found it beneficial to show my students additional possibilities for using Second Degree, therefore I usually teach for a day and a half, or two full days with a larger group.

First and Second Degree are the practitioner levels. They cover every aspect you need to integrate, in order to become proficient in applying this ancient healing art. No further "boost" is needed to empower yourself spiritually.

Third Degree is only for people who want to teach Reiki, and should not be considered until a student has completed at least three years of not only self-treatments but, additionally, hundreds of treatments on others—ideally in a clinical practice or similar situation.

Third Degree is not meant to be taught in a seminar or divided into 3A and 3B. (There are no "half masters!") I personally will only train master students after I have known them and worked with them for at least a year, and who have at least three years of experience behind them. The master training is a one-to-one procedure and generally takes a full year to complete.

In addition to the three years of experience with Reiki, a Third Degree or master student should ideally have completed some self-assessment work beforehand. My own Third Degree students are required to take the Core Empowerment Training at least three times to help quiet the mind and prepare them to become teachers (refer to my book *Core Empowerment*, Full Circle Publishing, New Delhi, 1998).

I consider the master/student relationship, at Third Degree level, to be a lifetime commitment for both parties and, therefore, do not take it lightly.

11. How many Degrees of Reiki are there?

Reiki, the Usui Method of Natural Healing, was conveyed to the modern world by Mrs. Hawayo Takata. To more easily convey the various attunements of Reiki, she divided Reiki into Three Degrees.

The First Degree attunes or aligns the student to the Reiki frequency through four empowerments. This allows the student to experience a direct connection with Universal Life Force Energy so that they can begin to channel the energy to themselves and others. After a period of adjustment and a lot of practice on self and others (minimally three months), Second Degree can be conveyed. One attunement or empowerment is given, and three symbols are taught, which enable the energy to transcend time and space.

At the Second Degree level, distant treatments can be shared with others, but an emphasis is put on healing personal (emotional and mental) wounds from the past. As old past hurts are healed, a new self-confidence emerges, which helps to release protective ego-related patterns.

Third Degree is the teaching level of Reiki and should only be considered after a minimum of three years of practice—and this only if there is a strong desire to become a Reiki teacher. The focus of the Third Degree attunement is not so much on amplifying your healing power, as it is on empowering you to convey the attunements. There is one attunement and one symbol learned in the Third Degree training, plus the procedure for the First, Second, and Third Degree attunements. Generally Third Degree is taught over a one-year period. The student organizes and co-teaches several classes and has regular consultations with the master.

Ideally, at the Third Degree level, the commitment between master and student is for a life-long relationship, based on respect and the full awareness that, at the deepest level, there is neither master nor student but only Universal Love and Life Energy at play with itself.

12. Why are there Degrees?

The Three Degrees essentially correspond to three different combinations of attunements that energetically promote different shifts or openings. Although they are interrelated as one organic whole, the Three Degrees serve different purposes. The first set of four attunements in First Degree is to be given in close succession and then integrated for a period of at least three weeks. To absorb fully what you have learned may take a few months. The one attunement for Second and Third Degree each also need time for proper assimilation.

There are several distinct steps in the integration of Reiki. After the four First Degree attunements, the body/mind goes through a 21-day cleanse process. A period of self-treatment (and preferably a number of treatments on others) is desirable to help the student gain confidence in the treatment process. Although the energy is palpable during the First Degree class, the human mind, which is beset with doubt, easily forgets what it has experienced. Thus, consistent daily practice in the first few weeks is needed to gain confidence, because for many, simply learning to touch the body and listen to the hands can take some time.

If Reiki treatments are given on a daily basis, the life force energy continues to increase gradually over time. The next attunement can then be better integrated.

The attunement into Second Degree is much more fully appreciated after an extended practice at the First Degree level. Second Degree, which includes one attunement, also needs to be fully integrated before the Third Degree attunement can be given (if one desires to teach Reiki).

Basically, the Three Degrees delineate three distinct processes which each need time to be fully assimilated by the individual. Although there are basic guidelines to be followed in terms of time and practice between Degrees, occasionally there may be exceptions to the rule.

Some people actually find it helpful to wait a few years between First and Second Degree, in order to allow the practice of Reiki to work to its full benefit. Some may never even consider Third Degree, because they are content to apply Reiki, but have no desire to become Reiki teachers. The point here is that it is important to follow the voice of your heart and not succumb to any outside pressure that tries to convince you that you need Third Degree in order for your Reiki to become more "powerful." The truth is, there are many First and Second Degree practitioners who are more mature in their practice than others who now call themselves Reiki masters.

13. Why is there a fee for Reiki?

In order to help students appreciate such a "pearl of great price," and to ensure that people who take First Degree are actually motivated enough to use it, Mrs. Takata always encouraged an exchange of energy regarding Reiki. It is very similar to going into a doctor's office, where you pay a fee for medical advice. If you have paid hard-earned money for your advice, you are much more likely to follow it.

After giving many Reiki treatments for quite some time, according to Mrs. Takata, Dr. Usui noticed that many people took the results for granted and did not really take responsibility for their own health (much like many people who want an instant pill or cure-all from a doctor, but who will not correct the bad diet or lack of exercise which caused the problem in the first place). People generally paid the equivalent of a doctor's visit for a Reiki treatment (Dr. Usui was, after all, a healer with a wife and two children).

To help people learn First Degree Reiki, so that they could take better care of themselves, Mrs. Takata accepted or charged the equivalent of a week's worth of labor. For Second Degree, she accepted the equivalent of a month's worth of labor and, for Third Degree, the equivalent of a year's worth of labor. After such payment, people were no longer beholden to her and could gain the most benefit.

Today, unfortunately, many people have turned Reiki into a business and have no concept of the rationale behind charging for Reiki. Some give it away for practically nothing, in order to be "competitive," with the result that the students often don't appreciate what they have received. Others, due to their charisma and popularity, charge exorbitant fees yet teach low-quality classes in which their students are given little or no time to learn how to practice simple and straightforward Reiki.

Over the past 15 years, there has been much controversy in the Reiki community about the issue of the correct fees. At this point, there is no need to add fuel to the fire, because to the intelligent observer, the question of the right fee resolves itself. Reiki empowers you to become healthy and whole through applying the very energy you are actually made of. If you take this statement as a fact, you'll ultimately cherish the gift of Reiki and be willing to pay for it. On the other hand, if you don't even have an inkling of the depth and potential of the Reiki energy, then taking a Reiki class is probably not a good idea for you anyway.

Also, nowhere did Dr. Usui himself state that the exchange of energy has to be made in hard cash. You can be creative and think of other forms when they are called for, such as a work of art, a piece of jewelry, or certain services. However, I would strongly suggest that the teacher not become the banker for the student. The exchange of energy should be completed before the attunements are given, to avoid any source for future conflicts.

The bottom line is that, whether looking for a class or a treatment, discernment is needed. It is best to look for quality in the practitioner or teacher.

Chapter 2

FIRST
DEGREE
BASICS

*D*oubt can arise when we begin a new practice or healing technique. This often occurs because there is an element of unfamiliarity left that can undermine our ability to implicitly trust both ourselves and our own actions. Self-doubt and lack of confidence are the first obstacles that we need to clear away, if we wish to proceed along the path of Reiki. Thus, every new practitioner has to face the challenge of venturing into uncharted territory. The questions and answers in this chapter are intended to assist you on your journey and make it clearer and easier. They can help you gain the confidence and attentiveness to detail you will need for the proper application of the Usui Method of Natural Healing. If you have not started practicing yet, this chapter gives a good overview of the subtle and sometimes not-so-subtle phenomena you can expect, should you ever decide to receive the attunements and begin your own practice.

14. What is First Degree Reiki?

First Degree helps you to align with Reiki energy so that you can channel it to yourself and others, for the purpose of healing, through the simple laying on of hands. It helps put you in touch with the direct link you've always had (but never realized) to all the energy you'll ever need to heal yourself by calming the mind and raising your life force energy.

Because for thousands of years we have been conditioned to believe that we are not good enough, that we don't know enough, and that all we need is outside of ourselves, we've developed an acute sense of separation or subject/object relationship with reality. If you look around, you will see this for yourself. Everything in human society seems to confirm that we are terribly alone and very much lacking in one thing or another. This only amplifies our sense of neediness so that we begin to seek outside of ourselves to fill the vacuum.

Basically every single ad in magazines or on TV reminds you of what you don't (but should) have, whereas in reality, deep down, you *are* unbelievably rich; you are the universe itself with all its inherent wealth, although not in the ordinary ego sense of these words. We tend to forget that, in actual fact, all is energy, that even our bodies are a certain vibratory frequency, that indeed everything is vibration, and that there is no solid matter. Thus there are really no separate entities or selves and we are already totally connected to all knowledge.

Who we really are is the ocean of consciousness itself. Each one of us, who seems so separate due to the information our five senses give us, is very much like a "separate" wave in the ocean. There is an appearance of a lot of different waves, but actually, *all the waves are the ocean itself* and totally inseparable. Each one of us is like a wave who has forgotten who we truly are, and because of this forgetfulness, we also don't experience our true nature.

First Degree Reiki helps remove one of the veils of forgetfulness, so that a palpable connection is reinstated with the unlimited energy of the universe. At First Degree level, there may still be a sense that Reiki comes from the outside to heal the body and calm the mind. With practice, over time, a recognition dawns of a healing of a far greater scope than simple physical ailments. This healing will gradually remove a sense of separation and bring you to a direct experience of unity.

15. How many attunements are there?

In First Degree Reiki there are four attunements. The focus at this stage is to fine tune the physical vehicle, to actually raise the life force energy at a cellular level, so that the body can receive or channel greater quantities of life force energy to both itself and others. The purpose of the attunements is not to open chakras or awaken the Kundalini, although sometimes certain openings may occur. The focus of First Degree attunements is to reinstate the Reiki channel, the direct link we've always had (but could not perceive due to our conditioning) to the Universal Life Force Energy which we truly are.

The attunements can be given one per day, throughout a four-day period, or minimally, over the course of two days with 24 hours between the second and third attunement. Never should all four attunements be given in one day! If they are, this is a dead give away that you are not receiving the Reiki empowerments as passed down by Dr. Usui.

The first empowerment attunes the heart and thymus, on both the physical and the etheric level, and establishes the Reiki channel. The second empowerment affects the thyroid gland and, on an etheric level, helps to open the communication center. It also raises the life force energy of the nervous system, which then needs time to adjust. The third attunement affects the pineal gland (which, etherically, corresponds to the Third Eye) and the hypothalamus, which rules the body's mood and temperature. A sense of calm or peacefulness often occurs after this attunement. The fourth empowerment is the final "sealing in" process that sets the channel in so you'll never lose it.

All four attunements have an effect on the entire endocrine system and continue to impart their benefit during the 21-day cleanse process, as much of the dross in the blocked areas is let go of.

Your Reiki channel may "atrophy" over a period of years, if you don't use it, but it will always remain with you, ready to be reinstated whenever you call upon it, once all four attunements have been completed.

16. How long does it take to learn Reiki?

Taking a Reiki class is not like any class you've ever taken. There is nothing intellectual about First Degree Reiki, so there are no books to read or tests to take. Because it is totally experiential, it is very easy and enjoyable to learn (my youngest student was four years old). Within a two-day period, most people can assimilate the basic hand positions and begin practicing on others, as well as on themselves. After the attunements reestablish your connection with Reiki, it is then a simple process of learning to listen to your hands so that you will know how long to keep them on each position on the body.

17. How often should I practice?

Ideally you can treat yourself every day, morning and evening. I generally give myself a treatment when I lay down in bed at night, starting with the head and throat. I often just make it to my heart and fall asleep. In the morning when I wake up, I start where I left off and continue down the body, then sit up to do my knees, feet, and back.

For First Degree students, I also recommend that you treat seven different people, three times each, for the first 21 days after the class. This helps you gain more confidence in your ability to feel and share Universal Life Force Energy, as you receive feedback from others. Furthermore, as you give Reiki treatments, you also receive a treatment indirectly, for the energy has to flow through you first before being drawn through your hands into the other person; a certain amount, as needed, remains with you. The mind also tends to settle down more quickly with the extra practice and makes your self-treatments easier.

18. What are the basics taught in a First Degree class?

After receiving the four attunements of First Degree, you are taught all the hand positions that cover the endocrine glands (which correspond to the major energy centers, or chakras) and all the major organs.

Every Reiki teacher shares the background of Reiki with an in-depth history of Dr. Mikao Usui. Most also cover information on Dr. Usui's student Dr. Chujiro Hayashi and Hayashi's student Hawayo Takata, who brought Reiki to America and Canada, and from there, to the entire world. Most Reiki masters today can trace their lineage through Mrs. Takata.

An overview of First, Second, and Third Degree is given, along with all the essentials (many of which are answered in this book) regarding treatments. The five principles are also discussed, and there is always sufficient time for one or two extended question and answer sessions.

Most of the course however, is devoted to hands-on practice: self-treatment, group treatments, and giving and receiving at least one full-body treatment with a partner.

19. What is the structure of a First Degree class?

First Degree is organized in four separate four-hour segments. Some teachers share the attunements over four successive evenings. Most teachers, however, lead Reiki classes on the weekend, for the convenience of their students, usually from 9 a.m. to 5 p.m., with two morning and two afternoon sessions. The first session usually covers the history and background of Reiki, the hand positions for self-treatment, the first two attunements (if the class is given on a weekend), and self-treatments. There is usually a lunch break, and the afternoon is a long session of group treatments with a question and answer session.

On the second day (in a two-day class) the morning begins with the third and fourth attunements, more group treatments, and a discussion of the Reiki principles. After a lunch break, each participant has the opportunity to give a full-body treatment to a partner and then receive a treatment from the same partner. Generally, there is a group discussion with question and answers at the end of the class.

20. What are the hand positions and how can I treat specific ailments?

Every position on the body is a possible Reiki hand position, so there are no set rules of what can and cannot be treated. Ultimately, Reiki energy will always be drawn where it is most needed in the body, so there is no need to worry about putting your hands on a "wrong" position. With this all stated notwithstanding, there are some basic positions on the body which were recommended by Mrs. Takata to be covered in a full-body treatment. Her main focus was to treat all the major organs and the endocrine system.

I generally recommend that students either purchase or borrow from a library a good anatomy picture book, in order to learn the proper placement of the major organs and endocrine glands after I first demonstrate them in the class. Mrs. Takata never discussed treating chakras, which has become popular today (perhaps partially due to my book *Empowerment Through Reiki*, written 16 years ago, which was the first to discuss the chakras and their treatment at length), but emphasized the importance of the endocrine glands, which control the body's chemistry and happen to be in the same position as the seven main chakras or energy centers.

To begin a treatment, I generally start at the head, which helps to immediately calm the mind and release stress. I start by placing my palms over my eyes while simultaneously covering the sinuses and third eye or pineal gland. I next place my hands on the temples, ears, and then occipital lobes at the base of the skull. For the fifth position, I place one hand over both occipital lobes and the other over the forehead. This position releases headaches, stress, and tension. The next position is one hand over the throat and one hand behind the back of the neck. You then simply continue placing your hands in a straight line down the front of the torso, beginning with one hand over the thyroid, at the hollow at the base of the throat, and the other hand just below it, over the thymus, which is midway between the thyroid and the heart. Next, I place both hands over the heart, then both hands over the solar plexus, then navel, then belly, and finally ovaries for women (placing the hands just above yet touching the pubic bone) or inguinal nodes for men (focused toward the gonads) when treating another. Men should treat the gonads directly during self-treatment, because it helps prevent prostate problems. After the "circular headband" positions on the head, and the straight line down the center, you can then treat the liver (to the right of the solar plexus), the spleen/pancreas (to the left of the solar plexus), and the upper lungs (these last positions form a perfect square). I teach the positions this way to make them easy to remember, but they also can be given in a different, more systematic order. Thus, the student need only remember: a circle around the head, a line down the front, and a square at the top and bottom corners of each rib cage.

Mrs. Takata placed a lot of importance on covering the heart, lungs, spleen, pancreas, liver, gallbladder, large and small intestines, and so forth, on the torso, after first completing the head. I complete treating the front of my body by letting Reiki be drawn into my knees and feet, then begin on the back by treating my shoulders. With careful placement of the hands, you can then treat your own kidneys, adrenals, lower back, and sacro-iliac crest. When treating another, you can, of course, cover more of the upper back.

To treat specific ailments is quite simple. Mrs. Takata always recommended a basic full-body treatment, if you have the time (and if you believe you don't, it's good to make time), in order to support the whole organism and put everything in balance. She would then do an extra 30 minutes on the problem area. For example, in the case of a tumor, she would treat directly over the tumor. In the case of arthritic joints, after a full body treatment, she would treat for an additional 30 minutes on the affected joints. For asthma, she would give extra treatment to the bronchial tract and so on.

It is essentially basic common sense: you give a minimum of an extra 30-minute treatment to the affected area. In addition, I suggest giving extra treatment to whatever position drew a lot of energy during the full-body treatment, or to spots that felt particularly cold. Disease in one area of the body can sometimes be related to energy blocks in other areas, and through the vehicle of the full-body treatment, you can easily discover them.

21. How do I know when to change positions?

Very simply, after three to four minutes, if there is no significant energy drawn, you will probably get an intuitive sense to move on. Because the body is warm throughout, it is natural that, overall, you will often feel a certain equal sensation of warmth.

Occasionally though, your hands may feel additional warmth, or even a hot tingling sensation or pulsation, or even an intuitive sense that the energy is being drawn. When this occurs, you want to leave your hands on that position for a longer period, until the sensation seems to dissipate. As long as you feel increased heat or sensations, this means an increased amount of energy is being drawn. This is why you want to keep your hands in this position until the sensation decreases. Also, one common occurrence is that when you are treating someone, he or she will very often take a deep sigh (almost like a sigh of relief) when a certain position is complete. You can then move on.

If you find a cold spot, you may want to remain longer until the energy block "melts" and it begins to draw heat. Then wait until the drawing of the energy again seems to dissipate somewhat.

Overall I do not suggest timing the hand positions or necessarily treating particular positions for specific ailments. It is best to simply follow the body's own needs as revealed by the sensations in your hands, or a more subtle knowing (or instinct) which just tells you when one position is complete, thus a certain physical sensation is not absolutely necessary.

22. How long does it take to do a full-body treatment?

In my First Degree classes, I give my students 40 minutes on the front and 20 minutes on the back to complete one full-body treatment. This is mainly due to my own time constraints. I have found, over the years, that when I treat people without watching the clock and simply follow the messages in my hands, my full-body treatments seem to average anywhere from one hour and 15 minutes to an hour and a half. There is no harm in giving a longer or a shorter treatment. It all depends on the body's needs. Furthermore, if needed (such as in the case of cancer or AIDS), several treatments every day may be called for.

23. Is it okay to just treat the area that really needs it?

Yes, of course, everything depends on your own time constraints. Overall I encourage my students to simply trust their own intuitive abilities, to trust that first impulse in the moment, which is usually correct. Although full-body treatments with additional Reiki in the specific problem area are the ideal, when you have only a short time, Reiki given directly to the affected area is always beneficial.

24. Can I take on the other person's negativity or illness when I treat them with Reiki?

With Reiki, it is virtually impossible to take on another person's negativity or illness—or for them to take on yours. During other forms of energy healing in which you use your own reservoir of electromagnetic energy and transmit it to another, this might occur. Reiki, however, is Universal Life Force Energy, which is channeled and drawn *through* you, not *from* you. From this, you can logically conclude that the other person doesn't take on any of your personal energy patterns (physical or emotional "stuckness") and, likewise, you don't take on theirs.

Occasionally you may treat someone who, for example, may be repressing a lot of grief and sadness. If you happen to hold similar emotions in your own body—in other words, something in you is resonating on the same frequency as in the other person—you may start to process your own grief or sadness.

It is important to remember that, as you give a treatment, you simultaneously also receive one. Consequently, you will sometimes feel joyful and refreshed after giving a treatment. At other times, you may feel tired or somewhat down, especially if you haven't had enough rest or if you begin to process some of your own previously repressed feelings. A consistent feeling of tiredness may also denote a low-level chronic depression, which may not even have been recognized as such. Depression is not a feeling in itself, but a repression of feeling. Such repression generally manifests as a feeling of fatigue or tiredness in the body. The body may then actually need to sleep off all the density of the stuck feelings, and Reiki treatments will act to induce the rest that is needed. The other way to deal with these feelings is to simply feel them fully, consciously. (See *Abundance Through Reiki* and *Core Empowerment* for further clues on how to deal with stuck thoughts and emotions.) Ultimately, Reiki always gives you exactly what is needed to create balance, both in yourself and others.

Another point to consider is, naturally, when you sit in the presence of another person, if you are open or sensitive, you may feel his or her feelings. Also, if you are very empathic (have the ability to truly feel with another), you may even perceive their physical pain.

These sensations are transitory however, and will quickly pass through the body if you approach your treatments on others with the attitude that you are there solely to support them in their process, (not to play the great "healer"). If you do not identify with the concept that you have to heal them or make them "better," such sensations will simply pass through. These sensations can be viewed as practical diagnostic tools which help you discern where to focus your attention during a treatment.

A simple way to deal with empathetic sensations of another is to thank the universe for the information and then say "cancel, cancel, cancel." By acknowledging the sensations and not resisting them, they can be easily dissipated. When we say "cancel, cancel, cancel," we let go of any identification with the sensations, further acknowledging their transient nature by not allowing them to become a "problem" to be fixed.

25. What do I have to do to make sure that Reiki flows?

The only thing you have to "do" to make Reiki flow is have the *intention* to share it. Reiki basically happens on its own, as soon as you create the intention. Once it is flowing, there remains nothing to be done except to simply listen to your hands, because they let you know, through the sensation of heat, tingling, pulsation, or an intuitive knowing, that the energy is still being drawn. For the few people who have very little kinesthetic sensitivity (are not feeling-oriented, but may be more aurally or visually oriented), I always recommend a lot of practice on many different bodies, in order to develop kinesthetic sensitivity. Through the feedback from many others, you will eventually develop your own special sensitivity and know just when the energy is actually being drawn and when it has ceased to be drawn. Likewise, you will sense exactly when the time has come to change positions.

26. What should I think about when I give a treatment?

Once you have formed the intention to share a treatment and have begun the process, there is nothing to think about. Reiki is a listening process. Because Reiki just happens of its own accord, you ideally become like the captain of a ship who adjusts his course according to all the weather signals he receives. In the case of Reiki, the signals are either the sensations you feel in your hands and on your own or the other's body or sometimes just an intuitive sense that it is time to move on to the next position. There is a basic course you follow, but at times, you will just know that you need to stay in one position longer than in another.

For beginners who find it difficult to simply listen, because the mind is still very active, focusing on the attitude of gratitude (one of the five Reiki principles) is very helpful. You can focus on gratitude for being able to act as a channel of Universal Life Force Energy for either yourself or another. You can then translate this attitude into your entire life as you go about your day. An attitude of gratitude fosters a very positive outlook on life. Many benefits accrue as a result, for as you focus on gratitude for what you have, you continue to stay in the state of having (rather than not having).

If you are distracted by too many random thoughts, don't resist them, simply allow them to pass through. Let them appear and disappear of their own accord. Don't argue with them. As you put all your attention on them *without trying to make them go away*, you'll be pleasantly surprised at the result.

27. Can I hurt someone with Reiki?

Absolutely and unequivocally, NO! As Reiki is *drawn*, not sent, you do not really "give" Reiki; you only act as a vessel for the exact amount that the other person draws, as needed, through your channel.

It is very important to understand this, because occasionally you may give a person a treatment who seems to be in perfect health, but who, after the treatment, actually feels worse than before. Very often, people have problems brewing under the surface that they are not aware of, which Reiki brings to the fore to help heal.

In other words, Reiki can seem to exacerbate a problem before it gets better, because it sometimes can create a short healing crisis, much like any of the natural healing arts that act to support the immune system and not suppress it. Once, after doing a long lower-abdominal Reiki treatment on an old friend who I knew had suffered from ovarian cysts years before, I received quite a surprise. Later that evening, she ended up in the emergency room of a local hospital in dire pain. As it turned out later, she had kidney stones she hadn't been aware of. The Reiki treatment, having accelerated her life force energy, had acted as an assist in passing the kidney stones and put her into a painful healing crisis. Such incidences occur occasionally, so it is important to remember that you cannot actually hurt anyone in the sense of doing harm. Reiki only and always helps to bring balance and healing, albeit sometimes through a healing crisis.

28. Can I give too much Reiki?

Because Reiki is always *drawn*, not sent, you can never "give" too much Reiki. It is the idea of "giving" a Reiki treatment that creates this kind of misunderstanding. The body/mind of the recipient always knows instinctively what it needs and draws in just the right amount. No thinking is involved with either the Reiki channel or recipient during treatment, as Reiki far transcends the mind. Only the mind can worry about "giving too much Reiki."

The only thing that is necessary on the part of the person channeling the treatment is attention or awareness focused on the hands or on a sixth sense or intuition that just tells you when a position is complete. Even if you leave your hands on a position longer than the energy is drawn at a certain place, you can do no harm because the energy is, again, only *drawn* in the amount needed.

29. How long should I leave my hands on each position?

There is no set amount of time to leave your hands on any position. Essentially, if you have the time available, you should keep your hands in each position for as long as the energy is drawn. This could be three to five minutes or, in some positions, even 30 minutes. It sometimes takes two to three minutes just to begin to feel the energy being drawn. In cases where chronic ailments are present, such as a severely rheumatoid arthritic joint, it may take even

5 minutes or more before the energy really begins to be drawn, and then you may experience intense heat or tingling for quite some time.

The key is to decide which positions on the body are most important to cover in terms of treatment, in the time you have allotted.

30. Why is it that someone occasionally may feel worse rather than better after a treatment or even jittery or nervous during a treatment?

Sometimes when receiving a treatment, old feelings that have long been suppressed may come up and make a person feel antsy or nervous. This happens more often when treating men, who are unfortunately conditioned to suppress their feelings. As well, hyperactive or aggressive A-type personalities often are overcome by a sense of uneasiness during their first treatment. The best thing to do then is to simply suggest that the person put all his or her attention on the jitteriness or uneasy feeling, allowing it to be there, without resistance. Continually direct the individual to just keep noticing the feeling (until it simply dissipates). However, do *not* tell him or her that it will dissipate, because this would set up the expectation that the sensation will disappear, which in and of itself, is resistance to the jitteriness; it would then just become more entrenched.

In cases when actual physical pain is evoked, this is an indication that something has been there all along, but just had not yet surfaced until the time of treatment. Further treatments should then be given to help heal whatever has been brought to the surface. If the pain persists even then, a medical checkup is in order.

31. Should I pray or do a mantra or some ritual before beginning a treatment?

It is helpful, before beginning a treatment on either yourself or another, to quiet your own mind. Although the act of sharing a treatment will eventually quiet the mind in and of itself, it is good to get into the habit of centering yourself so that you do not continue to dwell on the chattery thoughts that typically possess peoples' minds. Whenever you are lost in your thoughts (identified with them), you are basically fast asleep, because you are dwelling in memory, so you are disconnected from the present moment.

The practice of Reiki on oneself or another helps to bring you out of a state of unconsciousness and into the present. People who are used to prayers or mantras may find them helpful to center. Another useful way to center is to simply draw your attention to your heart. The centering meditation in *Empowerment Through Reiki* is very helpful in drawing the focus away from the usual busy thinking mode right into Heart.

Another way to quiet the mind and connect with the person you are treating (even if it is yourself) is to begin noticing his or her breath and begin to breathe in synchronization with him or her. This helps to put you in the proper listening mode for Reiki and helps to pacify the mind.

32. What should I focus on when treating myself or others?

The development of an attentive listening mode is the most essential ingredient for increasing your acumen as a Reiki practitioner. As was mentioned in answer to the previous question, centering at the very beginning of a treatment will help put you immediately in an attentive, wakeful stance. Bringing your attention to your heart for a couple of minutes and then shifting your attention to the other person's breathing, eventually breathing with them, is a good way to begin.

There are several benefits to breathing in synchronization with the people you treat. First of all, it helps you to feel their feelings; it builds a sense of empathy as you begin to align with their energy patterns. In addition, because you are actively focused on their breathing, your own mind goes quiet and you can better sense their needs. Another benefit of synchronizing your breathing with the other person is that all the micro movements your hands make while touching the individual fall into synchronization with his or her own subtle body movements. (All of a person's body movements are synchronized with the breath.) A sense of oneness occurs to the degree that the other almost always forgets your presence and falls into a deeper sense of relaxation very quickly.

Overall, the most important focus to develop during Reiki is pure and simple awareness of what is. By using Reiki time as an opportunity to practice being present, the mind becomes increasingly quiet. A strong sense of peace and quiet then begins to carry over into the rest of your life as well. Stress decreases, and worry that is related to future and, thus, past concerns begins to dissolve, as you are more and more drawn into the present. Whenever you are focused in a true present, "dis-ease" is totally absent.

33. If Reiki is mainly for self-treatment, why do you ask beginning students to do so many treatments on others for the first 21 days?

It is true, the best gift you can give to yourself or the planet is to work on yourself. When you are happy, it is easier for those around you to also be happy or free of stress. The reason why I stress to my students the importance of treating many others in the beginning is partly to gain clarity about the efficacy of Reiki. Once you receive verification from all the people you treat, even if, at some later time, weeks or months go by and you find that you haven't made time to practice, you will have no trouble taking it up where you left off. You, in effect, will have no doubt about your ability to convey Reiki.

The other very important reason to treat other people in the beginning, in addition to doing your own self-treatments, is that our mind's subject/object relationship with the world makes it easier to focus on another person (an outside "object") and have your mind go quiet enough to notice what is happening in your hands. Typically, beginners complain of not noticing so much happening when they treat themselves as when they treat another. This is because we are so used to identifying with our chattery mind and its outward-directed focus.

Most people find it difficult, at first, to lay their hands on themselves and just listen. They get distracted by the mind, as it begins to think about all the things that didn't get done that day or what needs to be done tomorrow. In truth, many people are fearful of just focusing on themselves and being quiet. They are often fearful of feeling long-suppressed feelings and desires. By working a lot on others in the beginning, many of these worries get treated automatically, and it then becomes easier to just be with yourself and enjoy Reiki in peace and quiet.

34. What is the 21-day cleanse process?

It takes about 21 days for the body/mind to assimilate the attunements after each of the degrees. Because the attunements raise the life force energy on a cellular level, in addition to opening the Reiki channel, often physical toxins are released as well as "toxic" emotions. In other words, the body/mind is released, of its density as it shifts into a higher vibratory frequency. None of the adjustments should be feared, as each person only experiences what he or she is ready for. Overall, there is a sense of lightening of energies on both a physical and mental level.

35. What are some of the reactions to the attunements?

Most people feel a deep sense of relaxation during attunements. In a few, tears flow as many feelings are released from the heart. Occasionally people may hear or see things such as sounds or colors, but there is nothing to be afraid of. I always advise my students also not to be disappointed if various phenomena do not occur, because this is definitely not important. Psychic phenomena or powers are never an end in themselves. If they were, they would only serve to inflate the ego beyond proportion. What is important and easily palpable after the attunements is the amount of increased energy that is drawn through the hands.

36. Why do you ask us to keep a journal for the first 21 days after receiving the attunements?

During the 21 day cleanse process, a quickening occurs in the body/mind. As the life force energy is shifted to a higher, more loving frequency, what you have previously experienced as negative or dense thoughts and emotions are released. It is beneficial to keep a journal at this time to record whatever occurs.

It is important that you do not censor what comes up during your spontaneous diary session. Remember, the point of journal writing is *not* to describe beautiful events and happenings. You only have to write down what is passing through you at the moment, as truthfully as you possibly can, without embellishment and with all the feelings and emotions this evokes in you.

Journal writing helps draw your attention to the old patterns that come up so they can finally be let go of. Very often, the simple act of noticing one's own emotional or mental patterns rising up and the ego then acting them out diminishes their power over us with time.

37. Why do you recommend writing down our dreams during the 21-day cleanse process?

In addition to keeping a journal of the various things that happen to you during the day and most especially your reactions to them—it is also helpful to record your dreams. Dreams are a wonderful reminder for helping us get in touch with what is hidden in the subconscious mind. The subconscious mind carries many of the aspects of ourselves that we tend to forget or unconsciously deny. In order to effectively "lighten our load," it is helpful to bring these hidden aspects into full awareness. On many spiritual paths, including the Native American and Tibetan traditions, conscious dreaming is considered a direct way to full realization.

Due to the acceleration of the vibratory frequency of the body/mind, as a result of the attunements, many revealing dreams occur. To recall your dreams, it is helpful to give yourself the suggestion every night just before you retire: "I will remember my dreams." Say this three times to yourself each night before falling asleep.

The first week you may only remember your dreams once or twice. By the second week, you will remember them almost every day. It is important to write them down immediately upon awakening, so keep a pen and paper right next to your bed. What is most important to note is your reaction to the events in the dreams. For example, when a man dreams about a woman, the woman most often represents some of the man's own feminine aspects. Similarly, when a woman dreams about a man, the role the character in the dream plays, speaks of issues she is dealing with in regard to the male aspects in herself. (You can also view the approach you take to the opposite sex in your daily life in the same way.)

Although some dreams can seem very abstract, it is still important to note them. If you review your dreams after a month's time, you will begin to perceive certain patterns in them. Intuitive insights will occur as you begin to get in touch with parts of yourself which have long called out for recognition. However, it is not only negative aspects which are revealed; what often arise are positive features that we are afraid to acknowledge due to false or negative conditioning.

You can also continue your dream journal after the 21-day cleanse process is over, as well as your daily self-treatments. This will support further self-observation and an increased awareness, leading quite naturally to a further refinement of your energy.

38. Is Reiki only for sick people?

Most definitely not. On the contrary, Reiki is one of the best preventative "medicines" on earth. It is recommended that you use it with the attitude of maintaining health, rather than waiting for something to go wrong and then administering treatment. Of course, if you or a friend or relative fall ill, Reiki can be used to amplify the life force energy and induce healing.

Reiki heals indirectly by calming the mind and raising the life force energy. Because all of us suffer from some form of mental stress or physical discomfort, if used frequently, Reiki will eliminate the cause of stress which generally leads to physical illness.

Chapter 3

THE FIVE PRINCIPLES

*E*thics is an important consideration in all of our social interactions and especially in regard to any system of healing. In Reiki, the so-called "5 Reiki Principles" cover this aspect. However, they are remarkably different from what we would normally expect as guidelines regarding the usual do's and don'ts that society impresses on our behavior. In our own culture, we are accustomed to guidelines being delivered from "above," in the form of commandments or similar authoritative pronouncements. They are often loaded with numerous *shoulds* and *have tos*, which burden us with guilt and obligation. The Reiki principles suggest a rather more self-reliant approach. They come in the form of commitments or promises that we take on voluntarily—but not in the sense of "forever," like a sacred oath that we promise to observe until the end of time. Instead, we simply make a promise to ourselves that we will follow them "just for today." By always staying in the present moment and being with what is happening now, our commitment to this precious gift of life is renewed each day. Unburdened by the weight of false obligation, a freshness and vitality begin to permeate our life.

39. What are the five principles and where did they originate?

As a true Bodhisattva who sought to relieve people's suffering, Dr. Usui gathered wisdom from different sources to help people at different levels of maturity. As a general measure, Dr. Usui adopted the five principles the Meiji emperor had given to the Japanese people to help improve the quality of their lives. Dr. Usui probably recognized the spiritual nature of the emperor's principles and how, if used wisely, they would remove the cause of suffering and disease.

In order to change a person's situation in life, there has to be a change in attitude, for whatever you think, you will become. One bit of additional information I always share with my students is the fact that the universe is very generous; it will always prove your beliefs true. So beware of what beliefs or concepts you adopt!

If followed faithfully, these principles will lead to a more positive outlook on life because, although at first mere concepts and beliefs, they are totally wholesome and life affirming when integrated. With a shift to a better attitude, greater abundance in the sense of a feeling of deep satisfaction and well-being is most often the result.

40. The first principle is: "Just for today I will be in the attitude of gratitude." What does it mean? How can the attitude of gratitude affect my life?

If we foster the attitude of gratitude until we become gratitude itself, life becomes a never-ending expression of abundance. Whenever we concentrate on what we don't have (as many human beings do), we continue to experience the state of not having. Even if your life is currently, to all appearances, in a "negative" or down cycle, if you gather your resolve and begin to focus on all of the good things in your life—your family, the beauty of nature, your education, your talents, and so on—a shift will begin to occur.

The greatest challenge is to maintain the attitude of gratitude when things are not going well. My own remedy is to thank the God Force for allowing me to experience the body/mind's karma now rather than in the future. Besides, a sense of humor will get you everywhere!

Also, don't forget to be in gratitude when things are going well, because it is important not to become complacent and take things for granted. When you use gratitude with a sense of wonderment for the miracle of life that you are, you will stay forever young (even when the body/mind gets old or is cycling disease).

41. The second principle is: "Just for today, I will not worry." How can I keep from worrying? How will freedom from worry affect my life?

Worry is a signpost which shows how stuck you are in the ego and its attachment to having things its way. It is one thing to have concern about our loved ones, about taking care of business properly, and so forth, but it is quite another to find that you are incessantly in worry mode. If this is the case for you, it is time to take stock, for you have essentially lost your faith and trust in the universe; you have forgotten who you are.

To worry is to forget that the body/mind is only an actor in a play which has always already been written. However, this doesn't mean we should just sit back and let life "do it to us." As a matter of fact, we *are* here to *participate* (with enthusiasm). Most of all, we are also here to enjoy and learn from the character we are called upon to play. Once we realize we are the dreamer or the playwright him- or herself, all worry ceases.

Worrying over the past is futile. It is important to remember that each person (including yourself) does the best they can with the knowledge and life experience they have accrued in any given moment. Each person is a product of their conditioning. If you regret something you've done in the past, feel your remorse fully until it dissipates, simply apologize, and move on. Do not get into guilt or let anyone else lay that on you. Know that you act according to your resources, be thankful for every lesson, and let go. Give everyone else the same credit.

Worrying about the future is also a total waste of time. There is a motto that I adopted 16 years ago and still live by: *Expect the best in life, and when you receive something you didn't expect, know (trust) that it is the best in your present situation.* All of life's occurrences are only situations magnetized by the body/mind to learn from. Your body/mind has karma, but because you are not the body/mind (and thus do not have karma), what is there to worry about? Simply stay quiet and observe the one who worries.

42. The third principle is: "Just for today, I will not anger." Does this mean that I should suppress my feelings? How do I avoid getting angry?

Anger is another signpost that you are hooked by the ego. Anger arises when the ego notices things are not happening its way. Ironically, the best way to deal with anger is *not* to suppress it. Instead of getting angry at yourself for being angry, just stop and observe your anger (without trying to make it go away). Allow it to be there and just put all your attention on it. You can even imagine it as the ball of energy that it is and allow it to expand. Because your anger has a limited energy field, eventually it will dissipate. However, never try to use this technique with the intention of getting rid of the anger; it won't work. The moment you want to get rid of it, you will then be resisting the anger. And as we all know, whatever you resist, persists.

Anger is simply another bad habit of the nonexisting ego. It comes up when there is fear. The best way to dispel it in another is not to react to it. (This does not mean ignore it, because that is also a reaction.) When someone attacks you verbally, it might be better to ask them (with genuine concern): Are you okay? Did you have a bad day? Rather than going unconscious, taking the attack personally, and reacting back automatically, you can instead observe the fear in the other that has caused the anger to arise. You can also do the same when your own anger comes up.

When anger arises, it is important to feel it fully and not judge yourself for it or make it wrong. Repressing anger or rage only causes tumors or depression. By feeling it fully and putting all of your attention on it, without trying to make it go away, we ultimately take the charge out of it.

43. The fourth principle is: "In your daily work, be honest (true) to yourself." How are we supposed to understand this?

This principle is essential, as it points out the importance of spending your time wisely in such a way that is true to your own heart. It addresses the need to choose a vocation that helps you grow, and provides you with a sense of fulfillment. It also infers that you need to speak your truth wherever possible and not be afraid to ask for what you need (even though there is always the chance you may get rejected). Eventually, you'll get it.

To be true to yourself also speaks to each individual's need to draw the bottom line, to not let others invade your emotional and mental space (sometimes even physical space) without your permission. Most important, it also addresses every person's need to take time for themselves. To be quiet and to enjoy your own company periodically, without interruption, is essential for maintaining a peaceful existence. Only *your* heart knows what is most appropriate for you. Thus, you need to honor its message, which only is audible in stillness, when you are quiet.

A walk in nature, meditating, time alone practicing an instrument or hobby, or even daily self-treatments, can become that special time to just be by yourself. Ultimately, the more we are willing to give to ourselves, the easier it will be to give to others in a natural, heartfelt way. Life is simpler when we are true to ourselves.

44. The fifth principle is: "Just for today, I will be kind and respectful to all of creation." What does this mean? What are the ramifications?

Due to quantum physics, science has finally grasped the fact that not only are living beings—such as humans, animals, plants, and trees—vibrant and dynamic, but so are rocks, minerals, air, and water. In a direct sense, everything in creation is alive.

When students in my class ask me how it is possible to give Reiki to a car or a toaster, I always point out that cars and different forms of machinery are simply extensions of our own bodies. The body itself is our vehicle for expression in this world (even though we ourselves are not the body), which is directed by the consciousness that we truly are. The tools we use regularly even take on our etheric energy and become extensions of the body. Did you ever notice how your car, computer, or toaster have the tendency to always break down when you are in a negative mental cycle, when everything seems to be going wrong?

This is because, in effect, we are all telekinetic like Uri Geller, who bends spoons with his mind. After tuning in and bending a few spoons with my own mind years ago, I got the point. When we are out of synchronization mentally (because we are not listening to Heart) everything around us, including the physical body, suffers. Love is the dynamic force that truly runs the universe. It is our choice to notice and act on it.

Grace is always present, just waiting for us to receive it. The best way to tune in with this Grace is to begin by being kind and respectful to ourselves and then allowing the effulgence of this Love to emanate outward to all those around us and to creation itself.

45. How can I best use the five Reiki principles?

After I received the First Degree attunement, I used the first principle during every treatment I shared. I focused on the attitude of gratitude for being able to act as a channel to support another. So many positive shifts occurred in my life after First Degree that it was easy to focus on gratitude while doing self-treatments. This became my time to focus on and appreciate all that is good in my life. I feel that, as a result of this focus, an incredible amount of Grace began to flow; or a better way of putting it would be to say that I then began to notice (and thus manifest) what had been there all along. Even if challenging or unpleasant karmic episodes would arise, I now had the Grace to handle them with equanimity.

With the other four principles, I found it handy to put one on my bathroom mirror each week, just to remind myself to notice when I became angry, worried, and so forth. I recommend changing the principle on the mirror each week, otherwise it begins to blend in with the scenery and you just go back to being unconscious.

The key to these principles, is that they can be used as powerful wake-up tools, but you have to pay attention to them.

Chapter 4

ALL ABOUT
HEALING
WITH REIKI

*W*hen we start to get really involved and use Reiki more frequently in treating ourselves and others, inevitably a whole slew of questions are likely to arise. The purpose of this chapter is to address as many specific issues connected with the treatment of both acute and chronic problems as possible. However, it is also helpful to remember that Reiki is not designed to treat disease in the same manner as allopathic medicine, which is based on the (some scientists say *false*) premise that there is or will be one specific drug for every ailment. Instead of focusing on a specific disease, Reiki focuses on the fundamental health and goodness of the underlying energy of our embodiment and works to rekindle and strengthen it. It would, thus, be contradictory to the holistic spirit of Reiki to assume that there should be one specific hand position for every ailment. Instead, in the Usui Method of Natural Healing, we usually focus on treating the entire body/mind, before we turn our attention to any particular problem area. We focus on the underlying health of the entire system. In other words, we strive to nurture the environment in which health can naturally predominate, rather than being consumed with what might have gone wrong within it.

46. Is Reiki more than a healing method?

Yes, due to the ability Reiki treatments have to calm the mind, Reiki can be the first step toward realizing Self or inborn divine nature, in effect liberating the practitioner from limited states of being. With the true motivation of a Bodhisattva, Dr. Usui was inspired to create a simple system so that all lay people could treat themselves and each other. It is clear that he followed the main motivation of his family spiritual tradition, which is direct realization for the sake of all beings. In order to be able to work on oneself and realize the ultimate, good health and a strong mind are required.

It is difficult to attend to spiritual growth and development if your attention is focused on a sick or disabled body/mind. It is no wonder then that the synthesis of this ancient teaching, which Reiki is, deals with maintaining and/or regaining physical and mental health.

47. How does Reiki affect the body/mind?

What is transmitted is a form of pacification by the laying on of hands. Energy is passed on that helps to pacify, heal, soothe, and even energize the recipient. However, the activity of healing is not in a direct manner. Reiki addresses healing only in an indirect manner, by increasing the body's energy, relaxing the nervous tension of the body, and pacifying the upsets and imbalances.

48. How does Reiki affect chronic problems?

Most pathologies fall into either of two categories: acute or chronic. Chronic problems, by definition, are physical or psychological symptoms that have gone on for quite some time. When you treat chronic problems, it may take a while before you feel the energy being drawn. Usually, after a few minutes, a strong heat or tingling may be felt in the hands, and in the case of painful arthritis, for example, the person often describes a sensation of the pain rising to the surface and diminishing.

With chronic cases, people generally feel a whole lot better after one or a series of at least three treatments. Generally a healing crisis happens much later or not at all during an extended course of treatment. If a healing crisis does occur and the person describes an amplification of the problem, it is a good idea to do extra treatments at that time, because this is a sign that the last vestiges of the disease are being released, and Reiki will speed up the process. In my first book, I referred to this type of occurrence as "physical chemicalization," because in effect, the body is burning up whatever are left of toxins connected with the disease.

49. How does Reiki affect acute problems?

Acute problems are, by definition, of short duration— something that has just risen to the surface and made itself painfully known. Ideally, an acute problem should be checked out by a qualified physician or naturopath immediately; however, if none is available and you are "it," it is best to know what to expect.

Often, when dealing with an acute problem using any kind of natural medicine, including Reiki, treatment may initially exacerbate the pain (as usually the person is already in pain) rather than give immediate relief, as in the case of chronic problems. With acute conditions, Reiki sends so much powerful healing energy to the problem, Universal Life Force Energy will often be experienced as an irritation rather than a comfort.

It is important to realize this so that, if a person complains, you can help soothe them by letting them know that this is actually a good sign that they feel a stronger sensation, as it shows that a lot of healing energy is being drawn. In acute problems, the pain will usually dissipate within two to three days. Again, it is important to remember that acute problems often produce more intense symptoms during the initial healing phase, so you can let the person know beforehand, which enables them to adjust psychologically.

50. Do I have to remove my jewelry or clothes to either give or receive a treatment?

Some suggest it, although it is not a requirement. Because Reiki is Universal Life Force Energy, as is everything else manifest in creation (including clothes and jewelry), how could Reiki block itself or interfere with itself? Some books have filled peoples' minds with a lot of nonsense about Reiki. In other forms of therapy, such as Polarity, it is important not to wear jewelry, but as Reiki is not magnetic (although it flows within magnetic parameters), there are absolutely no seemingly solid objects that it will not flow through. Reiki energy cannot be interfered with.

51. Is it okay to cross my legs or for a person receiving a Reiki treatment from me to cross their legs?

There are no hard and fast rules about crossing limbs while treating with Reiki. Generally, I discourage people from crossing their legs or putting the hands behind the head while lying down, because both of these positions denote a protective stance.

One of the main purposes of a Reiki treatment is to calm the mind and help the person to feel their feelings. To feel your feelings, it helps to be in an open, "vulnerable" position. Crossing your legs while lying prone is a sign of discomfort or fear of vulnerability. It is actually helpful for the person to notice and feel their vulnerability. By putting all their attention on it, allowing it to be there, it will simply go through and disappear. My entire book *Core Empowerment* alludes to the true strength which lies in an open, vulnerable heart, which is contrary to what most of us have been taught.

When you remain true to Heart, in open vulnerability, you cannot be deceived and neither can you be manipulated to unconsciously and blindly serve another's purpose. In other words, true to Heart, you will always fully live out the Truth that Heart is. You will not bend others to your will, but you will also not be subservient to theirs.

52. How long does it take to heal various diseases, and can I guarantee results?

There is no set amount of time for healing any disease and absolutely no guarantee of results with any form of medicine, including allopathic treatments. All healing is pure Grace and just happens when the time is right. The best we can do when assisting others in their healing processes is to see them as totally perfect as they are (even if they have a disease) and trust that whatever processes they are going through are perfect for them, as it is all part of the learning process in life.

If we have a strong attachment to healing someone with our method (or any method), we actually do a disservice, as this sets up resistance in the other to receiving the healing. On the other hand, it is important to convey a clear and sure confidence to an ill person that he or she *can* indeed be healed. This is the greatest support we can ever give anyone, and is a sign of a true healer.

Taking into account the previous statements, there are average healing times for different diseases, but these are affected by the person's body/mind karma, which is an unknown, and by the person's willingness to change bad eating habits, and/or deal with long withheld emotions.

For example, in almost 50 years of clinical experience, Mrs. Takata noticed that small, marble-sized tumors would often disappear during two weeks of daily treatments (full body treatments, combined with an extra 30 minutes on the tumor). Mrs. Takata also recommended a change in diet, and a lot of freshly prepared carrot, beet, and celery, juice along with the treatments.

Basically, she found that if a body part (for example, as in spinal surgery) hadn't been surgically removed or messed with, sometimes even paraplegics could be healed. It really all depends on the person's openness to being cured. Ultimately, it is foolish to guarantee any kind of results. No doctor ever does. It is one thing to say with conviction: "You can be healed." It is quite another, to give guarantees.

53. What is the optimal number of treatments to give another?

Mrs. Takata always insisted that, whenever you start treating another person, you should try to give at least three treatments in a row. The first treatment seems to bring a lot to the surface on either a physical or emotional level. The second treatment acts to clear a lot out. The third leaves the body vibrant and filled with Universal Life

Force Energy. It is good to do the three treatments over three consecutive days or, minimally, within a week's time.

Of course, if someone is suffering from a chronic ailment which has gone on for a long time, there will most likely need to be a longer series of treatments in order to see lasting results.

54. How long should I treat someone?

Basically, as long as they need it. After you have practiced Reiki for a while, you will begin to get an intuitive sense with people of how long they will need treatments, and you'll be able to make suggestions at the beginning as to how many (approximately) they'll need. Overall, chronic problems that have gone on for years may require weeks or months of treatments, whereas acute problems may only need a few.

Another factor determining how long a person will need treatments is noticing if they are willing to give up the bad habits which contributed to creating the problem in the first place. For example, as in arthritis, are they willing to give up coffee, tea, dairy products, and meat? If they have emphysema, will they quit smoking?

When people refuse outright to make necessary changes that are related to the causal factor of their problem, I am very blunt in telling them that, although Reiki may make them feel better for a while, they should not expect a complete cure from it or from any other form of medicine if they continue with their bad habits. One thing Reiki may help them with, though, is giving up the addictive habits or habit which led to the disease in the first place.

Something else needs to be taken into account as well: every once in a while you may work with a person for a long time who just doesn't quite get healed. It may be that the person is receiving some sort of secondary benefit from the disease (such as the attention they have long craved for) or that they are purely riding on your energy. If you sense someone is becoming codependent and the healer-healee relationship is no longer healthy, it is wise to disengage and gently, yet with supportive input, send them on their way. I usually tell such a person that I have assisted them in every way possible and that my intuition clearly tells me that the last step is up to them. I boost their self confidence with a great deal of encouragement but clearly cut any apron strings of dependency.

55. Why should I charge for treatments or ask for an appropriate exchange of energy?

In Reiki, the cost is usually referred to as an exchange of energy. Considering that money and all other forms of exchange are basically different manifestations of energy, this is actually an accurate description.

Because Reiki is "a pearl of great price," it is important that it be appreciated (so that it is utilized). The first form of exchange of energy is to simply ask for something (to ask for help). This is necessary so that you are then open to receive what it is you need. Although it is hard for many people to accept this, the truth is that almost everyone is attached to his or her suffering and, in some way, does not really want to let go of it.

The "nonexistent" ego often prefers what it is familiar with, even if it happens to be a form of suffering. One example of this trend is people who choose one abusive spouse after another or the person who dramatically tells you their troubles and tales of woe with a gleaming smile on their face. A person may, in full "consciousness," claim to want to change, but their actions, as they constantly go about sabotaging their happiness, often negate the claim.

I am not a cynical person, only a practical one, as I am sure Dr. Usui was. At a certain point, after spending years helping people who only profess to need your help but lack the capacity and openness to really receive it, you begin to focus on the ones who really want it and are able to use it.

The people who seriously want help are, first of all, willing to ask for help (and really mean it), and secondly, they are willing to offer something in return. This doesn't have to be money, per se. In ancient times and, to some extent, still today, it can mean totally letting go of money, such as in the case of a sadhu. This would be an appropriate exchange of energy for a multimillionaire to whom a normal-sized fee would mean little or nothing. Giving up all attachment to wealth itself might be more of a challenge. With one of my students who did his Reiki master training with me, the exchange of energy was two exquisite and accurate copies of original Tiffany stained glass lamps, which took him two years to complete. The amount of work he put into the lamps really helped him appreciate what he received. They are incredible works of art and were truly a labor of love.

For most people, however, money is the most convenient exchange of energy, and there is no problem in setting an appropriate fee for what you have to share. The recipient will then more fully appreciate what you have to give them, and they are left free of a sense of obligation. The results they gain afterward are then dependent on their own effort.

56. What kind of exchange of energy should I expect for sharing Reiki treatments?

When you treat people in your family or close friends, there is already a constant exchange of energy established, so there is no need, and it is probably not appropriate, to ask for one. If a neighbor you don't know very well hears about Reiki and asks you to help them, you can always offer a sample treatment. However, it is wise to let them know it is best to have three successive treatments, and then perhaps ask for an exchange of energy in the form of a suggested donation to yourself or your favorite charity, some favorite food you like (that they can prepare), or some such thing. This leaves them free of feeling beholden to you, and will help them further appreciate your time and effort. They also gain more benefit.

If you decide to offer Reiki to the public, you can set an appropriate fee, or ask for donations according to each person's ability to pay.

57. What should I do if I don't feel differences in different hand positions on the body?

If it is only on yourself that you don't feel differences, this is related to the fact that it is difficult for most people to stay quiet and really focus on themselves. Most beginners tend to get lost in their own thoughts, as the chattery mind distracts their attention from what is happening in the hands. For these people, it is still appropriate to do a lot of treatments on others, until the quiet mind you develop when focused outward on another finally begins to have an effect when you work on yourself.

If you also don't feel any differences when you are treating other people, this is probably due to the fact that you are not kinesthetically oriented. In other words, you may be more aural or visual in your orientation and not so body sensitive, such as in your hands. If this is the case, I recommend also doing a lot of treatments on others. Although you may not notice differences at first, some of the people you treat will give you feedback, which will eventually clue you in to the variations in your hands.

Eventually, with practice, the synapses in your brain will begin to connect with the nerve endings in your hands, and you will begin to notice what may be, for you, subtle differences in different positions. Also, with practice, your intuitive sense will develop and you will just know when to move to the next position, regardless of any physical sensations.

58. How can I develop empathy so that I can sense more what another needs?

In answer to question 31, I described a way of breathing in synchronization with another that will help you begin to feel what another is feeling. Life revolves around the breath. When we are in our heart, we tend to breathe with full, deep breaths in the lower belly.

On the other hand, when we breathe shallow breaths in the upper chest, this can be taken as a clear sign that we are stuck in our heads and focused on our thoughts. Taking a few deep, full, belly breaths and consciously filling out the lower abdomen and lifting the rib cage just before beginning a treatment will help you to center and relax the mind.

We tend to tune into others better when we are focused in the heart and when we're in listening mode rather than thinking mode. True empathy (feeling with another) happens more easily when we are quiet and open to receiving rather than in a state of trying to figure out what another needs with the mind.

It is important to note the difference between empathy and sympathy, because too many so-called healers approach their "healees" with sympathy. Sympathy, or feeling sorry for someone because they have some awful problem or disease, does not honor them. In any case, it would be more accurate to say *thinking* sorry, for sympathy does not involve real and unfiltered feeling. Sympathy is insidious, because it is a one-upmanship game. In effect, you (as ego) put yourself above the other and feel pity for the "poor unfortunate creature" who is undergoing whatever they happen to be undergoing. Sometimes I want to gag when I see this missionary approach.

When you feel sorry for another and then buy into it, the other begins to feel smaller or not as good or capable as you. You actually help perpetuate their misery by supporting them in the victim role. You get to play "the almighty rescuer" and pump up your ego—while they continue forever to play the miserable victim. It is a sickening self-perpetuating merry-go-round.

Empathy, however, is something quite different. It takes a genuine open heart to feel empathy, because empathy involves the ability to truly feel with another (not think sorry thoughts about them). Practice putting your attention on the heart when you are treating and breathing with another, and you may begin to experience some amazing things.

When you approach each being with total equanimity, honoring their need to undergo whatever experience they are undergoing, the world takes on quite a different color. The secret is to turn this same approach around on yourself.

59. How can I protect myself against taking on another's pain?

The more awake you are, the more you also become sensitive to others' pain. At times, you may even feel their pain or emotions in your own body. The secret here is not to become identified with it. If you don't identify with it, it will simply go through. It is when you begin to buy into (believe in or identify with) the "big healer" role of believing you have to save the world (or even one person) and make him or her or the whole world *better,* that your problems start.

In actuality, the world is perfect as it is, even with all its many and blatant imperfections. We happen to be living at the end of the age of *kali yuga* (the densest of the four world ages), so sometimes it can get downright uncomfortable! The secret is not to be attached to feeling happy or sad, good or bad, but to notice the perfect silence behind all the noise of your mind (and of others' minds) and stay with that silence. You may then feel occasional unpleasant sensations pass through you as you move through your life, but they won't overwhelm you.

As you begin to develop greater sensitivity and first feel others' pain, you can thank the universe for the information (as it tells you where to place your hands or keep them longer) and then say, "cancel, cancel, cancel," so you remember not to get hooked on it.

60. Can I treat someone who is dying?

Absolutely. Sometimes the greatest healing occurs during the death process. As anyone familiar with the *Tibetan Book of the Dead* knows, the different *bardos*, or intermediary states, which begin at the moment of death and continue for 49 days, provide a rare opportunity for self-realization. Giving a dying person Reiki will help to calm their mind and give them an easier passage in a process that is not much different from birth. In fact, Reiki is also good for mother and child during the birthing process.

Once Mrs. Takata felt compelled to give Reiki to a friend's corpse, at the heart area, about half an hour after she had died. The woman came miraculously back to life just as they were bringing in the coffin to take her away! As I recall, the woman lived about five more years. Many amazing things have happened with Reiki. Whether it heals you of an ailment or helps you through a difficult passage, it is of great benefit.

61. Can Reiki be used with other healing methods?

Reiki stands on its own as a self-contained healing method. It does not need to be combined with any other technique to improve it. However, if you are already a practitioner of another healing art, you may choose to use Reiki with it. Many allopaths, homoeopaths, naturopaths, chiropractors, ayurvedic physicians, acupuncturists, and massage therapists have found Reiki to be very beneficial with their patients. Its soothing and calming effect helps quell a patient's worries, fears, and stress. The fact that Reiki raises the life force energy helps to indirectly improve the efficacy of any other healing method.

62. Will Reiki go through casts, metal, and other hard objects?

Reiki will go through *anything*. Because Reiki is what everything is made of, and everything is Universal Life Force Energy, there is nothing that it cannot penetrate. As substratum itself, it can be drawn through casts, metal, and all seemingly solid objects, because as we already know, there is truly no solid matter.

63. Can I give Reiki to my car, computer, toaster, or other inanimate object?

Because the different types of machinery we use are all extensions of the physical body, it is possible to give Reiki to them. Any clothes or objects you use constantly begin to take on your etheric energy or imprint. It has been proven scientifically that 99 percent of disease is psychosomatic, or caused by the mind. In truth, any disease (including accidents) is 100-percent psychosomatic.

In the same way that our mind affects the body, our mind also affects the machines we use all the time. Just notice how often your car or computer screws up when everything in your life (mind) has gone awry. There are no guarantees in healing the body, and it is the same with these inanimate objects. However, I have had great success periodically with cars and a few assorted gadgets.

Much like taking care of the body by using Reiki as preventative medicine, you can Reiki your car, boat, or computer to keep it in good shape. This is actually preferable to troubleshooting under pressure when you need to fix something that has broken down.

64. Can I do distance Reiki at First Degree level?

While Second Degree Reiki focuses specifically on distance healing and amplifies the life force energy to do so, there is no reason you cannot try it at First Degree level. In my doctoral dissertation, years ago, I quoted a study done by a cardiologist on 100 of his patients who received bypass surgery. Of the group (unbeknownst to them), 50 percent were prayed for and 50 percent were not. The group who were prayed for did remarkably better.

Recently, Larry Dossey wrote a whole book on the healing effects of prayer, called *Healing Words*. You can simply imagine a tiny image of the person in your hands and give them Reiki, because, in a way, the sharing of Universal Life Force Energy is a silent and very beautiful form of praying for someone.

65. How can I use Reiki to remove energy blocks from the body?

Occasionally when you are giving yourself or another person a Reiki treatment, you may come across a spot where the energy doesn't seem to draw, and it may even feel cool to the touch. This is generally a sign of an energy block, where a thought form and its corresponding emotion are stuck in the body. It is important to be aware that sometimes a point on the body may feel cool in relation to the heat in your hands, because, in actuality, the person is drawing a lot of energy. So you have to discern whether it is clearly an energy block or if your hands feel hot in comparison to the patient's body temperature because he is indeed drawing energy. Sometimes asking yourself quietly will evoke a simple yes or no answer, if you aren't sure.

Once you have determined that there is an energy block, by simply leaving your hands on long enough, the dense energy will begin to dissipate. If you have received Second Degree, utilizing the second symbol will help release the block. For First Degree practitioners, there is a simple technique I teach—a sort of short cut that is not a Reiki technique but that is derived from psychic surgery:

What you can do is scoop both of the hands together over the energy block and gather it into a tight compressed ball on the surface of the body. Grasp it with your left hand and raise it away from the body. Then sever it with your right hand by making a slicing motion, totally disconnecting it from the body. Imagine the condensed energy expanding for a few seconds, until it dissipates, letting it go totally, then replace your hand on the same position. You will be surprised at how quickly the energy will begin to draw.

66. Why are so many people attracted to Reiki today?

There is a great need in every sentient being today to raise the vibratory frequency of life force energy. It appears to me that we are living at a time when tremendous love energy is engulfing the planet as we shift into a new and higher vibratory frequency. Unfortunately, when this higher vibratory frequency comes up against all the density stored in most peoples' bodies, it can cause a lot of pain or discomfort.

Most people are carrying lifetimes of grief and anger that needs to come out and be released. Most feel drawn to this new energy and want to feel better at this higher frequency, but the higher frequency just acts to highlight their overwhelming sense of stuckness. This is one of the reasons we see so much strife in the world. Instead of safely pounding out rage on pillows, people are picking up guns to shoot it out on each other and adding fuel to the current ego explosion.

Fortunately, due to incredible Grace, Reiki has re-appeared; providing a simple easy tool to raise every individual's life force energy so that this new frequency can be received joyously. Reiki not only raises the vibratory frequency, it also calms the overly distracted and scattered mind, the very root of all fear: the ego. The nonexistent ego is turning rampant in its fear of extinction, in its "solid" sense of doership. With the Grace of Reiki and other such gifts, may it all implode with the ease of the Berlin Wall!

In short, people everywhere on the planet are turning to energy work such as Reiki, because they are fed up with the deception and lies that are fed to them day in and day out. There is a great need for genuine empowerment, and Reiki puts you in touch with its source: the heart.

67. What is the best time to do Reiki?

Anytime is Reiki time. There is no special time of the day to give "better" Reiki. It can be given before or after a meal, but it might be wise to let food settle a bit so that you have an opportunity to feel your feelings better. To make it easy on yourself, you can do self-treatments every night just when you lay down to go to sleep. I usually get as far as my brow and occipital lobes, or perhaps the heart, and then I fall asleep. In the morning I simply start where I left off; I sit up and do my knees, feet; and all the back positions.

It is helpful to do Reiki first thing in the morning and the last thing at night. You start your day with a quiet mind, and you finish in the same way.

68. What will happen to me after practicing Reiki for a while?

Most people experience a new feeling of vibrancy in their lives. The mind becomes less preoccupied, and a greater sense of peace is the result. I have had many grateful spouses tell me stories about a cranky husband or wife who, after a few treatments with Reiki, began to behave like a much more loving human being.

People who have been ill or suffered chronic problems for a long time often experience great relief, and many are completely healed of their ailments. Cigarette smokers often find out that their desire to smoke just disappears. Overeaters and drinkers also undergo a waning of their addictive behaviors as they are exposed to feeling their suppressed feelings that caused the addictions in the first place. These feelings then begin to be gradually released.

In the beginning, there may be physical or emotional cleansing processes, as the most dense energies are immediately sloughed off. However, these soon dissipate, as physical and subtle energies become more balanced.

69. What do I do if my life takes a bad turn after things have been going well for a long time?

This is a question I sometimes get from students who have used Reiki for three or more years. Things tend to improve immensely after the First Degree level, as so many old, negative patterns fade away. If Second Degree is used to its greatest benefit, by conditioning and doing distant treatments on old childhood traumas, the process of freeing up old behavioral tendencies continues.

At a certain point, for most people, a fear will arise that is something to the effect of: *What will happen if all my patterns disappear? What will be left?* This is an ego-based fear that arises the more deeply the mind goes quiet.

The ego is, in effect, the biggest "possession" of all—even more so than a ghostly possession. It is what keeps the body/mind coming back again and again in different forms on the wheel of life as it reincarnates itself over and over.

As you get close to real freedom, the mind goes wild, as it feels itself dissolving. It much resembles a dying fish in the throes of death, flopping all about. The more you get in touch with the unlimitedness of being, of that which you truly are, the ego can go manic (just observe the world today). As such, the ego doesn't even exist, as it is only a construct of the mind to help the body/mind survive in the world. Its fear of dissolution often gets projected on the outer world, and before you know it, things seem to fall apart for a while, as more of your fears manifest before you.

Because, by having seen through many of your patterns, you now have a more solid foundation, however, the fear eventually begins to recede. One way it can be dealt with is to keep a vigilant observance on the "one" who fears. Continuous self-inquiry will put the true culprit out of commission. For further handy hints on how to deal with this, the 42-day abundance plan in *Abundance Through Reiki* points out ways as to how to be vigilant in your daily life, and *Core Empowerment* gives you clues on how to live as Heart. Both of these books are recommended for those who want to live as Peace and Freedom.

70. Should I use crystals with Reiki?

There are no *shoulds* or *shouldn'ts* with the practice of Reiki. If you are drawn to both Reiki and crystals, you can refer to my first book, *Empowerment Through Reiki*, which describes a variety of ways to use crystals.

Crystals have been used for centuries in different healing and spiritual traditions. They act to amplify or maintain an energy vibration and are very often placed on the diseased area of a patient to help the body continue to draw energy.

Crystals act very much like batteries, because they can store energy and information and then send it out in an amplified form, which is why they are so much a part of modern information and other technologies.

71. How can I use crystals with Reiki?

A crystal is a geometrical formation of a fused mineral or substance, with molecules or atoms that are arranged in a repeating pattern. This gives crystals a symmetrical appearance. They have a stable geometrical and mathematical orderliness, which they maintain with extreme precision—a factor that contributes to their usefulness as a programming tool. In *Empowerment Through Reiki*, I mentioned how their capacity to form and hold a specific energy matrix and transduce information between the subtle levels, or planes of existence, is another key to their usefulness as a healing tool. In other words, their usefulness lies in their ability to work primarily on the subtle energy body.

Most "dis-ease" in the body manifests first in the etheric or energy body. We can perceive these blocks with Reiki when we come across a cool spot or an area that doesn't seem to draw energy. After treatment, you can charge a crystal and leave it with the person, to be used over the area that seems blocked. It will help to dissipate the blocked energy and charge the area with further energy.

The simple basics for using crystals are to clear or cleanse the crystal; to charge the crystal; and if you want to expand its capacity, to activate it. In addition, by focusing your positive thoughts, you can also program the crystal. The essentials are cleansing and charging the crystal, which I will briefly explain.

To clear or cleanse a crystal, you can soak it in a saltwater solution for 24 hours. Other methods include using running water or blowing on each of the facets while visualizing them as clean and pure. To charge a crystal with Reiki, simply hold it between your hands, with the intention of charging it, and then focus on the purpose for which you wish to use it. Then simply give it to the person who needs it, to carry in their pocket or to place on the special area that requires extra attention.

72. Is chakra balancing a part of Reiki, and if so, how do I do it?

Yes, indirectly. Mrs. Takata who brought Reiki to America, never focused on chakras, per se. What she stressed over and over again is the need to treat the entire endocrine system, as well as the major organs. It just so happens that the placement of the endocrine glands corresponds directly to the seven main chakras, or energy centers.

The endocrine glands, such as the pineal, pituitary, thyroid, thymus, adrenal, and gonads, keep the entire physical body in balance. Likewise, the crown chakra, Third Eye, throat, heart, solar plexus, belly, and root chakras keep the etheric or energy body in balance. Both the endocrine glands and the chakras act as transducers, transmitting energy back and forth to the physical and etheric bodies.

One of the great benefits of Reiki is that it works both on the physical and the etheric bodies simultaneously. Also, as you do a Reiki treatment and are open and sensitive enough to feel, you will pick up immediately if one gland or chakra is out of balance, because it will either draw an excess of energy in comparison to the rest of the body, or it may feel cool due to an energy block. Thus, a full-body Reiki treatment is really the best way to balance the chakras, as you'll feel just which area may need more energy.

If you wish to concentrate just on the chakras, you can even have the person stand sideways in front of you, and then put one hand in front and one hand in back on each of the main chakras, and slowly move from top to bottom over each of them. You can also have the person lay down. Occasionally, you may also get an intuition to put each of your hands on different chakras simultaneously, to somehow create balance. Just trust your hands and your intuition, and they will tell you what to do.

73. Can Reiki protect me from negative energy?

The more you use Reiki, the more you also raise your life force energy automatically. As you raise the vibratory frequency of both your physical and etheric bodies, dense or "negative" vibrations can no longer enter. One good example of this very phenomenon is the experience many of my Second Degree students share when they describe what has happened to them after First Degree.

After doing a lot of self-treatments and treatments on others, they notice that many old "friends" drift away and new ones appear in their lives. The new friends are happier, more positive people. Only the old friends who are also happy, positive people themselves, tend to stick around.

One of the greatest benefits of Reiki is that it slowly teaches you that there is ultimately nothing you ever have to protect yourself from. As you mature spiritually, you begin to understand that, in truth, there is no "good" or "bad," "right" or "wrong." There are only conscious people and unconscious people.

"Evil" deeds are done by people who are fast asleep, even though they may seem right on the ball and very cunning on the surface. If you are awake, with an open and vulnerable (feeling) heart, you will be able to sense the deep pain and anguish which drives people to hurt others. Although it definitely hurts to be on the receiving end, you will not take it personally, if you are truly aware of the other person's motives.

Another essential point you need to be aware of is that by buying into or accepting the concept that there are others from whom you have to protect yourself, you immediately assume that others are more powerful than you. This then enables others to lay power trips on you, as they sense your fear unconsciously and act on it.

Of course, there are brutes in the world of whom it is necessary to be aware, thus, you need to be vigilant all of the time—most of all for your own ego (which is what puts you in fear in the first place). Not even a magician of evil intent can harm a hair on your head, if you don't believe in his or her power.

With unconscious brutes who want to use sheer physical force, we need to learn to do some form of Aikido with them (that is, learn to deflect their energy, let it turn right back on them, or simply get out of their paths). Sometimes, when such people become too overwhelming, they have to be dealt with. Very often, it is best to baffoon them, to relegate them to their proper place. At that time, the superior intelligence of the heart will guide you. It will also tell you when the best thing you can do is confront them skillfully, without hurting yourself (by confronting them consciously without *internal* resistance).

74. How can I center myself with Reiki?

By its very nature, Reiki has a centering effect. In *Empowerment Through Reiki*, I shared a lengthy centering process which focuses the attention and directs it away from the head into the *hara* (or *ki* or *chi* center) in the belly. Because in this almost totally westernized world educated people tend to identify with the intellect and its limited capacities, it is important to learn how to reconnect with your feelings that give a truer sense of the situation at hand. In martial arts, the belly or naval chakra has always been the focus for centering.

Although it is helpful to center in the belly, or *hara*, these days I find my attention focused on the heart. To me, it is most important to stay centered at all times in Heart, with that which we all are. Heart, in this sense, goes way beyond the simple physical heart, or even the heart chakra. The Heart of who we truly are totally transcends all limits of time and space. At the Heart of who we are, time and space, as we conceive or know them, do not even exist.

As a human being with a body, it helps to connect first with the physical heart—to lay your hands on the heart chakra and give yourself Reiki. As the heart stirs and the mind goes silent, you will begin to sense the longing, your very own heartfelt desire for that which you truly are. From this still small point, there is no better guide or guru to the awesome nature of your real beauty.

75. Can I do Reiki if I am already doing other spiritual practices or forms of meditation?

Yes; Reiki does not interfere with any other spiritual practice. It can only enhance it by raising your life force energy and relaxing any stress or nervous tension.

76. Can I mix Reiki with other forms of spiritual practice?

It all depends on the practice. Some paths seem to be rather territorial and protective of their flock.

From the point of view of Reiki, there are no objections whatsoever. If the practice calls for a calm or quiet mind, and you need more energy to do your practice, Reiki will be beneficial.

Reiki actually can be used as a spiritual practice in and of itself. Daily practice of Reiki helps you become a more loving, heart-centered person, which, in essence, is the core of any spiritual practice.

77. How does Reiki affect meditation?

Reiki helps meditation by quieting the mind, which usually talks a mile a minute. Reiki in and of itself could almost be called a form of meditation because, with practice, it silences the overly busy mind very effectively. Also, because Reiki is Heart energy, it helps you become a more compassionate human being—both towards yourself and others.

To my students who are meditators, I often suggest that, while doing self-treatment, they focus or meditate on the one who wants to meditate. This particular type of inquiry, if done with strong intent, can end all meditation, because the meditator simply dissolves in direct self-realization.

78. Can I mix Reiki with other forms of therapy?

Reiki stands on its own as a complete form of treatment; however, it can be easily blended with different forms of body work or massage, rebirthing, and acupuncture or acupressure. It also works well with more mainstream forms of medicine. Psychologists may find it helpful, as well, as Reiki can help people tune in with their immediate feelings. Also, although I don't generally recommend talking during a Reiki treatment, if emotions come up that a person needs to discuss, you can talk and still give Reiki.

79. Will Reiki have an effect on the use of allopathic drugs?

Yes; people generally need lower dosages, the more Reiki treatments they receive. For example, doctors of diabetics who use Reiki very often find that their patients need less and less insulin. Also, doing Reiki helps remove the craving for sugar itself, which most often leads to diabetes in the first place.

80. Can I continue drug treatments while receiving Reiki?

Yes; the only thing is, you may need to monitor the dosage, because perhaps you will need less due to Reiki's indirect beneficial effect.

81. Do I need to change my diet when I do Reiki?

I only ask students for the duration of my First or Second Degree class to abstain from coffee, tea, alcohol, and heavy food. I also recommend that they minimize sugar intake, because all of these substances tax the body. Coffee, tea, and sugar are addictive substances which have a deleterious effect on the nervous system. Because the attunements or empowerments of Reiki shift the vibratory frequency of the body, toxins are often released very quickly. You are asking for a more intense 21-day cleanse process, if you keep putting toxins in your body. For people who are heavy tea or coffee addicts, I suggest "homeopathic" (smaller and smaller) dosages for a while. Going cold turkey (quitting too suddenly) could otherwise cause headaches and other cleansing reactions, in addition to the possible cleansing effects of the attunements.

As far as diet is concerned, that is your own choice. When people are sick with cancer I generally recommend Gerson therapy, which essentially is a raw food diet. The raw, live enzymes in raw vegetables and fruit act to boost the immune system. For example, even dogs, when they are sick, eat grass. Gerson therapy has been proven to heal cancer for more than 70 years. I actually healed myself of two tumors using it. The important thing is to make sure you eat or drink the freshly pressed juice of *organically* grown vegetables and fruit so that you don't put your system under additional stress from cancer-causing residues of pesticides.

The longest-lived peoples in the world include the Hunzas, Bulgarians, some tribes from the Caucasus, and the Mayans. What they all have in common is that they all eat at least 75 percent raw foods and often live to be 120 years old—some as old as 140! Most people today eat 95 percent cooked food; even if it is good vegetarian fare, it is still dead food.

If you want to maintain your youthful vigor, healthy raw salads, bean sprouts, and fruit are a good choice. Also, fasting twice a year, for at least seven days, on a combination of fresh lemon juice and equal parts of maple syrup or molasses or cane juice (no honey and absolutely no white sugar!!) mixed with water, you will feel truly rejuvenated. Refer to any of Paavo Airola's books for information on fasting.

82. Can I get rid of addictive habits, such as smoking or drinking, with Reiki?

If there is a strong desire to quit, there is an equally good chance for success. Paradoxically, I generally suggest to my Reiki students who really want to quit smoking, not to bother trying to quit. The desire to quit anything is resistance (to the addiction). You often end up smoking more because (as we all know) whatever you resist, persists.

Instead, what I generally suggest is to make a commitment to yourself to wait five minutes every time you get an urge to smoke (or drink) and then allow yourself to smoke later, if the urge is still there. Most often, what happens is that, in the five minutes you wait, the feelings you were avoiding by smoking come up and pass through so that the urge to smoke disappears. Treating yourself with Reiki also helps you to feel your feelings in a totally non-threatening way.

Basically, all addictions are a simple avoidance of feelings (see *Core Empowerment* for a more in-depth presentation of the connection between repression of feeling and addictions). When we learn to accept our feelings, often the addictions simply vanish. This has happened to many Reiki practitioners who found that smoking simply became distasteful.

83. Will Reiki cure overeating and help me lose weight?

Overeating, like all addictions, is related to not wanting to feel certain feelings. There are two main motivations for most human actions: to feel something or to avoid feeling. If you are very much overweight and do not have a serious thyroid problem, chances are Reiki will assist you by at least helping you to feel your feelings.

The next step is to look at your diet. If you use any hydrogenated oils or margarine, you need to relearn how to cook. Try steaming food instead of frying or boiling it, and experiment with healthy, unprocessed oils (and yes, butter, when needed). Grilled food is also less oily. If you cannot find a proper steamer, you can improvise with a steel colander in a larger pot. Add water to the pot until it reaches the steamer or colander, add your veggies, close the lid, and bring to a boil until they are still slightly raw.

The other handy hint for losing weight is exercise. When I'm on the road (which is a lot), I minimally do calisthenics: 200 sit-ups (start with 50 and work your way up), and 100 leg-lifts to the side, inner thigh, and lifting up from the back. At home, I do aerobics three times a week. I won't tell you how old I am, but I look and feel 10 years younger than most people my age. A little discipline does pay off.

Once you get into the habit of exercise, you'll never want to stop, because after 15 minutes of exercising, the endorphins (the natural feel-good "high" of the body) kick in, and all stress and worry simply disintegrate. Reiki, good diet, and exercise are open secrets to a healthy body.

84. Are group treatments helpful?

Group treatments are a wonderful way to get together and share Reiki. Because several people work on each person, a full-body treatment takes less time. Having a number of hands on the body also gives a great sense of comfort and support. I usually recommend that my students arrange Reiki gatherings, because it's always enjoyable to be treated by someone else or, occasionally, even by several other people simultaneously.

For these Reiki gatherings, I also recommend finishing all the conversations first and then turning on pleasant, meditative-style music to create a nice, quiet, and calm atmosphere, so that everyone is at peace and relaxed enough to feel the soothing presence of Universal Life Force Energy.

85. Can I treat plants and animals with Reiki?

Plants love Reiki, and I can attest to great success in my gardens, both in Washington state and in the tropics in India. You can simply hold your hands up, with palms facing the plant, and let it draw.

Animals also enjoy Reiki. I have treated many dogs, cats, horses, and even snakes (not the poisonous variety). Basically, you follow the same pattern of treatment on animals that you do on human beings.

86. Can I treat my food with Reiki?

It is very good to treat your food with Reiki. Simply hold your hands over your plate and let it draw. In the moment you Reiki your food, your mind also quiets down and it is easier to receive your meal to its greatest benefit. Treating food enhances it with life force energy that, unfortunately, most food is lacking these days, due to degeneration of quality from the approach of big agro business. Finally, when you have finished eating, you may also Reiki your belly to enhance the digestive process.

87. How does Reiki release old blocks and emotional or mental patterns?

Reiki helps you feel the feelings that lie behind all surface emotions and general behavioral tendencies. As we are enabled to feel our deeper feelings, old habits and proclivities simply lose their hold. They may still sneak up on us for a while (old habits die hard), whenever we are tired or cranky from not eating or overworking, but are soon dissipated through the willingness to simply admit them. With practice and simple noticing (vigilance), we begin to take our patterns less seriously. We begin to finally understand how automatic they really are, and consequently, compassion for both ourselves and others is the result.

Chapter 5

SECOND
DEGREE
BASICS

*A*t some point, we may feel the need to graduate from a focus on healing the body to one of healing the mind, which is in the domain of Second Degree Reiki. Second Degree addresses the psychosomatic nature of disease. Although as simple and straightforward as First Degree, the practice of Second Degree actually amounts to applied quantum theory, as it helps to render inactive all of our preconditioned and imagined boundaries of time and space. It is, after all, the boundaries of our concepts or conditioning that make us ill and throw us off balance. If used to the fullness of its potential, Second Degree Reiki can deliver much more than the ability to treat someone from a distance; it can anchor us in the unshakable awareness of the limitlessness of our being. It can accommodate the experience of the richness of existence, which generally remains covered up by the countless limiting beliefs we project on our own nature.

88. What is Second Degree?

Second Degree Reiki is the next step in attunement to the Reiki energy. In addition to a further empowerment, which helps to fine-tune both the physical and etheric (energy) bodies to a clearer frequency of Universal Life Force Energy, certain symbols are also taught which enable the student to let Reiki be drawn across time and/or space.

Through the use of the Second Degree symbols, distant treatments can be shared with others. Additional tools are also given, to enable you to use distant treatments on yourself to release traumas from the past. These old energy blocks, if not attended to, could still continue to affect you in the present. At Second Degree level, your awareness is amplified to help you focus your attention, so that you are enabled to address the root cause of disease: mental and emotional upsets.

89. How much or how long should I practice Reiki before taking Second Degree?

It is wise to use Reiki for a minimum period of three months. I even encourage my students to wait as long as six months and practice it consistently every day. After First Degree, it takes the body 21 days just to assimilate the four attunements. In certain (rare) circumstances, Second Degree can be given after 21 days, as I mentioned in *Empowerment Through Reiki*, but it usually is not in the student's best interest.

The First Degree attunements accelerate the life force energy. Using Reiki continuously every day on oneself and others helps to keep the process going. The longer you practice Reiki, the more you increase your vibratory frequency. Thus, the student who uses First Degree for a period of time will not only become fully familiar with its subtle nuances and be better prepared to use it, he or she will then also receive a proportionally greater boost with the Second Degree attunement.

Thus, three to six months minimum experience at First Degree level is recommended. It should also be noted that some people who have actually waited a few years to receive Second Degree have noted major openings as a result of their thoroughness and patience.

90. How many attunements are there in Second Degree?

In Second Degree, only one attunement or empowerment is given. It is usually shared at the same time that the symbols are conveyed.

91. How many symbols are taught?

At the Second Degree level three, symbols are taught to help create a bridge from the heart of the Reiki channel to the heart of the healee, through which the energy may be drawn. Even at the Second Degree level, it is a misnomer to say that you "send" energy because, indeed, this never happens. For this reason you can never invade someone with Reiki. On some level, the other person's body/mind has to be open to receiving the treatment, just as in First Degree hands-on treatments.

The first symbol is the absent healing symbol, which helps the individual create the bridge through which another can draw the energy. The second symbol, often called the mental symbol, is used to help eliminate the mental blocks that cause disease and stress in the first place. The third symbol enables the healee to draw a more amplified version of Reiki, as needed, according to the circumstances.

According to some unspoken guidelines of genuine spiritual transmission, certain symbols or procedures are never to be revealed to outsiders who are not practicing the same discipline. This is pertinent for the three Second Degree symbols, as well as their uses. They are not to be taught outside a Reiki class or printed in a book (although some people have done so, for their own reasons).

92. How long is a Second Degree class?

Mrs. Takata, the woman most responsible for promulgating Reiki in America, often taught Second Degree in only four or five hours. Although she always stressed the necessity for longer First Degree classes so that beginners left fully assured of their ability to convey Reiki, Second Degree with her was short and to the point. It was given only to students who had fully integrated First Degree. Essentially, she gave the Second Degree attunement, taught the three symbols, and conveyed the ways and means for sharing distant treatments.

My own classes are set in three approximately four-hour segments. In the first segment, I give the attunement and symbols. In the second and third segment, I like to share some of the ways I have used Second Degree for my own spiritual growth and development. I also like to give the participants the opportunity to try out Second Degree in the course of the class itself.

93. How does Second Degree Reiki differ from First Degree Reiki?

Whereas the attunements of First Degree tend to focus on amplifying the life force energy of the physical body, which also often sets off a lot of physical cleansings, the Second Degree attunement seems to have a more intense effect on the etheric or energy body.

Over the years, I have had a lot of feedback from my students about the heightening of their intuitive abilities. Also, quite a few have mentioned experiencing strong sexual feelings (caused by suppressed sexual energy being released). All of these are symptoms of old energy blocks in the etheric body opening up. Basically, the mental body becomes much more fine-tuned and, as a result, intuition is increased. Some people actually develop greater kinesthetic abilities or sensitivities, such as clairaudience, clairvoyance, and clairsentience. This enables us to follow our own inner guidance to a much greater degree.

As healers, we increase our ability to sense another's needs. Not only do we feel another's needs through our hands, additional more specific information may begin to come through intuitively, as well. At this stage, I encourage my students to allow themselves to let go of the specific pattern of treatment they learned in First Degree and follow any impulses which come through.

In general, a further letting go occurs in Second Degree, on an energetic level that increases the individual's awareness. It is important, at this point, not to get impressed with any newfound abilities (such as psychic abilities that may develop), as this will only set you back in your spiritual growth and development. Second Degree can best be approached as a further tool for waking up rather than something gained from outside of yourself to boost your power.

94. What happens in the 21-day cleanse process after Second Degree?

The results of the Second Degree cleanse process vary with each individual. There often are further physical cleansings similar to what can happen during the First

Degree cleanse process. Also, further emotional clearings take place.

What is most common is the gradual noticing of an increased intuitive awareness. For some it is very sudden and dramatic, as certain abilities abruptly open up. For most it is a gradual process, as they begin to notice, after some time, a greater sensitivity to those around them or enhanced perceptiveness in their daily lives.

The bottom line is that no individual ever gets more than she or he can handle. Openings in awareness only occur when a person is ready—when all unconscious fears have been sufficiently dealt with. The practice of Reiki at the Second Degree level will, itself, remove these fears.

95. How can I benefit most from Second Degree?

Second Degree's real benefit is the peace you feel after letting go of all of your old resentment, anger, and worry. Most people are initially attracted to Second Degree Reiki because they either want to increase their power and intuitive abilities or they are interested in learning how to do distant treatments on others.

The greatest gift you can receive from Second Degree, however, is freedom from the old mental blocks and patterns that would otherwise keep you in suffering (the kind of innate power you feel when freed of the ego's chains). The main focus of my Second Degree course is teaching my students how to do distant treatments on themselves. With the tools of Second Degree, you are enabled to go back in time and remove the sting of old traumas or painful memories that may still be affecting you in the present.

In all of the world's ancient Shamanic traditions, there have always been practices taught which would help the individual draw together all the fragments of self, all the buried incidents which hold sway over the personality, and keep one from experiencing true freedom. By bringing these incidents into full consciousness, acknowledging their lessons, and letting them go, we unburden ourselves of sometimes lifetimes of guilt and false obligation.

96. How can I use Second Degree on myself?

Once you have been initiated into Second Degree by a master in the direct lineage of Dr. Usui and have learned the proper Second Degree symbols, you can create a "bridge" across both time and space to incidents in your past which need healing.

Over a period of years, I worked with Reiki, bridging the energy to the time when I was in utero and then worked forward to the present. I worked with each year of my childhood, adolescence, and young adulthood, creating a bridge to myself in the past to which the energy could be drawn.

At first, I worked with incidents I could recall—especially any incident when I was unjustly treated or made by someone, out of ignorance, to feel small or "not good enough." Slowly but surely, through the Reiki energy, old limitations and negative beliefs and doubts I had picked up from others were methodically dealt with.

Although I have always been blessed with a pretty high degree of self confidence and very supportive parents, all the societal conditioning that brainwashes you into thinking you are not good enough, don't know enough, don't have enough, and so forth, began to be lifted off my shoulders.

With practice, the recollection of events became crystal clear; in each event where someone had tried to make me feel small, I could see his or her own unconscious inner motivation for doing so: deep unconscious beliefs in his or her own unworthiness. It became easier to not take people personally and also to not react back unconsciously out of a similar ignorance and insensitivity.

Slowly but surely, there was no longer a need to call up the ego to "protect" me as it became apparent there is no separate "other" to be protected from. As most of life's burdens were lifted, a sense of peace began to supplant my earlier self-confidence—a sense of peace not dependent on feeling good versus "bad," happy versus "sad," or even up versus "down"—just plain and simple peace and noncausal joy.

97. What is the real secret of Second Degree?

Eventually, after using Second Degree, for a period of years, to recollect and discharge the energy of old stuck patterns, you may discover its secret: that truly there is no time and space to traverse, that they do not exist! At the highest degree of understanding, time and space are actually only concepts which describe how a human being experiences all of life's circumstances in a linear fashion.

It is difficult for the human mind, with its attachment to the five senses, to comprehend that there is no past, present, or future—that in actuality everything is happening all at once. This is why, for example, the ancient Rishis in India, or Nostradamus in the west, could see into the "future." They simply had vast peripheral or panoramic vision.

After a period of years, as you dissolve a lot of the *attachments* you have to your beliefs and behavior patterns, as you get in touch with the noncausal joy that lies beneath all of your surface patterns, a major shift can take place. At a certain point, the entire illusion of time and space can fall away and leave you with a direct experience of Self. As each of the seeming memories of the past are recalled and brought into the present, the past literally shrinks until there is only one vast and limitless present.

In that moment, there is actually no "you" or ego left, for the experiencer simply disappears. Later, the memory or ego of the body/mind may remember that "something" happened and tend to claim the experience, but from then on, everything is not quite the same. The sense of the unlimitedness of who you truly are can then call you into the noncausal freedom that is now able to express itself through you.

98. How can I use Second Degree to do distant treatments on others?

After receiving the Second Degree attunement from a qualified Reiki master and learning the three symbols, you will be taught how to create a bridge from your heart to the heart of another, across which the energy can be drawn. Just as with First Degree, it is important that the person ask for a treatment.

However, you cannot "invade" someone with Second Degree Reiki, because even at this level the energy is *drawn*, not sent or projected. In cases, for example, when someone is in a coma and is therefore in no position to ask for a treatment, you can always create a bridge, begin the treatment, and notice if the person actually starts to draw energy. You will feel if they are drawing or not. If they draw energy, then you can continue the treatment. If not, you simply cease the treatment.

99. Why are the symbols and the descriptions of the attunements not to be published in a book? Are they secret?

Attunements can only be properly given by a person who has used Reiki for a considerable amount of time (that is, usually several years), and has fully imbibed the essence of Reiki so that it then can be passed on. Although there is a specific form or ritual to the attunements or empowerments, the form remains worthless, if given by someone without any energy or experience behind them, who has not fully embodied Reiki. It is much the same with the symbols for Second and Third Degree.

Some well-meaning yet, in my view, naive people have published the Reiki symbols and described the attunement process in books (most of these descriptions, by the way, are inaccurate). The authors of these books seem to think that just anyone can learn from a book what must actually be conveyed *directly* from master to student.

You cannot receive Reiki empowerments through a book, by correspondence, or over the Internet. The attunements must be given directly from one human being to another, and they can only be given by someone who is fully *qualified* and *experienced*.

Second Degree Symbols are only meant to be given to First Degree students who have a lot of experience under their belts and have developed confidence and trust in the efficacy of Reiki. A minimum of three to six months of experience at the First Degree level is important to fully gain the benefit of Second Degree.

Also, the Second Degree symbols will not work if you have not been attuned at the Second Degree level by someone who carries the essence. The point of not printing the symbols in a book or elsewhere is threefold:

First of all, you don't give a nursery school student high-school level information; they won't be able to absorb it. As Jesus said: "You don't cast pearls before swine." Secondly, Reiki can never be "known" or understood intellectually. It can only be *experienced*. You can indeed talk about it, but really only to relieve the mind's doubts. Head knowledge does not help you share better treatments or raise your life force energy. It often only creates more confusion if not laid out simply. Third and most importantly (which most of the people who have printed the symbols are unaware), although there have been a few power monger types in Reiki, as in all things human, for the most part the Reiki symbols and attunement procedures have not been held back or kept secret from anyone because an alleged "Reiki elite" wanted it so for the sake of their own power. It is purposely only shared with properly prepared students who are ready to use the symbols with the same intention as every practitioner in the long Reiki tradition.

It is important to understand that most human beings are entirely unaware of the power of the human mind. For example, in my Core Abundance Seminar, I always caution my students not to share their goals with others until the foundation is laid and they are well on their way to actually manifesting them in physical reality. If you share your ideas prematurely, others most often will (unconsciously) think: "Oh, so and so, he or she will never accomplish that goal or that project!" Because of these negative thoughts, the energy of your project will actually dissipate.

The average human mind, due to false conditioning, dwells often on the negative polarity, and exposing your ideas to such negativity will only dissipate the energy of your project. You also want to keep the energy *condensed*, so it will support you. I encourage them only to share their ideas with the few people around them who have a positive mindset.

The same is pertinent for Reiki. It has always been important to only share the symbols with people who are ready to use them with the proper intention. To show them to an unknowledgeable, doubting person (let alone a huge public) who might think, "What is this gobbledygook?" would only dissipate their energy. Fortunately today, however, Reiki is so widespread that ignorant negativity will probably no longer act to dissipate their power. There are just too many Reiki practitioners, all with the same positive intention.

Still, the proper attunements, which are received directly from a fully qualified master are the only way Second and Third Degree symbols or attunements have any efficacy. Thus, what is the point of publishing them except sheer greed, ignorance, or the naive presupposition that you can save the world with them, as if the world needed saving?

The world may indeed appear imperfect in your eyes, and doubtless, there is much strife. However, the approach to relieving this pain is to abstain from meddling in the affairs of others (except for emergencies, when your intervention is clearly called for), but rather invoke the absolute perfection inherent in all being.

You do not want to subject the symbols and attunements to the distortion of the outside world. You want to keep them hidden so that they can silently and miraculously transform the world into what it essentially already is: Awareness, Consciousness, and Bliss.

100. Does Second Degree amplify my power?

What Second Degree actually does is increase your body/mind's life force energy. Through the Second Degree attunement, the vibratory frequency of the physical body, with a special emphasis on the energy body, is boosted. As a result, you are able to channel at a higher (or lighter) frequency. Essentially, what you experience is a "de-densification," as more dense energy is let go of. This may make you feel more "powerful" simply because you are now much more in touch with what had always been available but that you previously couldn't access due to your having been stuck in beliefs, judgments, and limitations.

Chapter 6

THIRD DEGREE BASICS

*O*ne of the greatest hazards to the integrity of the Usui System of Natural Healing is a misunderstanding of what it means to be a "master." Most of us are in danger of confusing mastership with being someone else's master, whereas it actually infers the mastering of oneself and the taming of one's own body/mind. The idea of being someone else's master is the greatest fallacy and a reflection of what is wrong with our entire culture.

Most people still want to transfer responsibility for their lives to outside authorities—to their minister, priest, or rabbi; to their politicians or government; to their doctor; or to whatever authority is most convenient. There are always those who are willing to take this on for a fee—but at what cost? A lack of many individuals' responsibility for their own lives—as we see, if we care to have a look—creates a breeding ground for tyrants. Today we see countless emperors without clothes, who are empty, powerless, and even terrified of their own mortality internally, yet have managed to amass vast amounts of superficial external power, in order to compensate for this sense of hollowness. A large portion of humanity has succumbed to this machismo.

For Reiki, as for any other form of spiritual healing or practice, the identification with the trappings of false external power is tantamount to a mortal blow to its essence. A Reiki master is always accountable for his or her use or misuse of the teacher's role. It has never been so important for anyone either considering the role of a Reiki teacher or who is currently on that path, to review their own heart/mind and actions. It is essential to realize that the role of the teacher is actually the role of the servant who helps his or her students heal and points out ways to help them find their own essence, their own truth.

101. What is Third Degree?

Third Degree is effectively the teaching level of the Usui Method of Natural Healing (*Usui Shiki Ryoho*). At the Third Degree level, you learn one more symbol and receive the Third Degree attunement. You also learn how to convey the First and Second Degree attunements and how to properly organize and teach Reiki classes.

The Third Degree training takes, at least, about a year and should only be considered after a teacher and student have known each other through working together for a minimum of one full year. This way, the teacher can act as a proper mirror for whatever the student needs to learn, because a bond of trust has been well established.

102. Do I need Third Degree to increase my power?

Much like Second Degree, Third Degree is more about fine-tuning your life force energy (and not so much about amplifying your power). Unfortunately, what most people still don't understand is that, while First and Second Degree are about empowering you by putting you in touch with the direct connection you've always had but previously never realized, with all the energy there is, Third Degree is about dropping your desire and need for power. In other words, Third Degree is about dropping the ego's drive to be "better" or more "powerful" and to finally realizing that *you are* Reiki itself (so that all sense of separation falls off like a garment that has been outgrown).

If Second Degree is used to its greatest advantage for several years, its benefit will make Third Degree a moot point in terms of further "empowerment."

103. What should be my motivation for Third Degree?

The only reason for Third Degree is the intense desire to teach Reiki. If your idea is to "save the world," I would suggest first doing some deep self-inquiry to help put your missionary zeal in perspective. It is important to get in touch with what is ultimately real, so that you can discover there is no world (outside of yourself) to be saved. It is essential before teaching anything to first acknowledge your real motives (especially the subconscious ones) for wanting to teach. Once they are brought to full awareness, they can no longer control you and you won't tend to project them on others.

For example, some people teach in order to gain respect and love from their students, to control others, to boost their egos, and so forth—all of which are not serious problems, as long you are aware of them and can at least admit these tendencies to yourself and others. If this is the case, you will have half a chance to not fall for them (and if you do fall for them occasionally, you'll snap out of it quickly). Naturally, most people who desire to teach also have altruistic ideas about teaching; but to be a teacher who can actually help benefit students, you need to be aware of all the shadow aspects of your personality.

The whole point of teaching, from the standpoint of the teacher's own growth, is to empty the proverbial cup; it is to realize that truly there is no teacher and no student—there are only two human beings sharing the joy of remembering who they truly are. If this is your motivation, you'll be a fantastic teacher!

104. How long should I practice Reiki before considering Third Degree?

Because Third Degree is a training for teachers, it is necessary that you be equipped with a full knowledge of First and Second Degree through direct personal experience. It takes three to six months of using First Degree just to get a basic understanding of how Reiki can affect different people in different situations. This experience can only be gained by treating many different ailments. Furthermore, you need to imbibe the changes in yourself (which result from self-treatments and from treating others).

Second Degree provides a tool for releasing the charge of old, unnecessary mental and emotional patterns. Extensive work at this level is needed to not only disengage from your own ego identification but also to learn about the various ways Second Degree can support others. A group of the original masters trained by Takata, plus their first few trainees from the early 1980s, have all come to the conclusion that three years of experience is what is really necessary to be fully prepared to teach Reiki.

I myself tried teaching masters after only one year of experience. I found the results to be far from beneficial. Much of an individual's unfinished business seems to come to the surface, and then it is just taken out or projected on his or her students. Although three years of experience is my requirement or guideline, sometimes even that is not enough time. For some individuals, more time is needed in preparation for teaching.

Furthermore, not everyone asking for Third Degree may, deep down, really want or need the teaching level of Reiki but may make the request because, subconsciously, the need is for something else. In such cases, through empathic resonance, it is up to the teacher to uncover the real need and help the student by pointing out a way to fulfillment.

105. Is there such a thing as separate 3A and 3B master levels or a special training for grand masters?

Third Degree is always to be taught as a whole and not subdivided. There may be steps and stages in the teaching, but giving only the attunement to Third Degree as an end in itself and calling it "3A," is not recommended. This practice was started by one of the original Reiki masters who, as I understand it, went very much against her teacher's (Mrs. Takata's) wishes.

This particular master decided that she would give the Third Degree attunement and symbol to people who wanted to use Reiki only for their spiritual growth and not to teach. For people who wanted to teach Reiki, she would convey how to transmit the First and Second Degree attunements, but she withheld the process of how to conduct the empowerment into Third Degree. This she called "3B."

As has already been pointed out several times, Third Degree is not about amplifying your power; rather, it is about *dropping* your power trip and your attachment to the belief that you need to be powerful or have a powerful personality. Therefore, "3A" is redundant, because you can only gain the real benefit (and by this I mean spiritual benefit) of Third Degree when you actually start teaching and, in the process, begin to "empty your cup." Through teaching you actually put yourself on the line and your ego under the scrutiny of your students. In this way, your students will also become your teachers, which is a very healthy reality check. Basic common sense should also tell you that there can be no "half masters." Unfortunately, two of my own master students, who had been influenced by this renegade master, have contributed to the resulting confusion caused by this practice.

Courses in "grand mastership" are the height of absurdity because, in Reiki, there are no grand masters, and neither are there in any other truly spiritual practice. Hierarchical distinctions such as "grand mastership" always appear on the horizon when a live spiritual tradition is about to lose its freshness and begins to turn into a quasi-political religious organization. This can never be the purpose of Reiki, which essentially is an immediate access to the health and wholeness that you always already are. An ongoing experience of such immediacy would only be compromised, if subjected to the weight of dead hierarchies.

The lack of any hierarchies, on the other hand, places a lot of responsibility into the hands of each and every Reiki practitioner. Because there is no one above you to keep your ego in line, you have to open to intrinsic awareness, or the Energy itself, to guide your daily actions.

106. Can Third Degree be taught like a seminar or a class?

No, not ideally. Third Degree is a one-to-one proposition. Occasionally, I have worked with two or three people simultaneously for parts of their training, but it is necessary to give a Third Degree student a lot of personal attention.

The master/student relationship at Third Degree level is for a lifetime. It is also necessary that your master gets to know you for at least one year before actually starting with the training so that he or she can address your particular needs.

These fly-by-night "instant" Third Degree seminars are simply just money-making propositions. The modern tendency toward less and less direct human contact and interaction does not suffice with Reiki.

107. What are the requirements and preparation for Third Degree?

There needs to be a minimum of three years experience as a Reiki practitioner. This translates to daily self-treatment, plus plenty of experience working on many different people—preferably in your own Reiki clinic.

My own Third Degree students are required to have worked with me for at least one year, preferably organizing a few classes for me in order to learn organizational skills. Most of all, this time together allows us to develop a bond of trust, so that the student can really receive what I have to teach. I may also suggest other seminars or reading, according to each student's ability, to broaden their scope so they are better prepared for their own students' questions later on. Another thing I suggest is that my student audit other teachers' classes, just to get a feeling for different styles of teaching.

This initial relationship also enables me to get to know my student and all of his or her patterns and quirks, so I can better point them out. To further this end, I also require that my master students take the *Core Empowerment Training* at least three times to fully drop their attachment to teaching so that, paradoxically, they become better teachers. Any kind of self-assessment work or direct self-inquiry can also help to this end.

Thus the main requirements for Third Degree are: first, a strong desire to teach; second, the mechanical requirements of three years' experience, a broadening of scope, and a deepening of self-knowledge (to know and help others you must first know and help yourself); and third, an exchange of energy with the teacher, which can take many forms.

Ideally, the exchange of energy needs to be completed before the training begins and the attunement is given, as it is wise not to become your student's "banker." Also, the exchange of energy needs to be in keeping with the student's capability, yet also needs to stretch their limits to a large degree, to show that they are indeed in earnest. This is helpful, because it is necessary for a student to be really sincere to actually benefit from Third Degree. Thus for a multimillionaire student to whom money means nothing, you would have to become creative. You might have to come up with some type of service they could give to others or some other way they can actually share their time, which is often more precious to them than money. Although nowadays money is most commonly used as an exchange of energy, I have sometimes retained services or artwork from my students.

By much trial and error, I have learned to always write a contract with my Third Degree students so that everything is up front and later there are no misunderstandings.

108. How is Third Degree taught?

Third Degree has to be molded differently according to each student's needs. After all the preliminary preparation is dealt with and the exchange of energy is decided upon, the student and I choose a time to begin the first portion of the training. This usually consists of a number of days together, during which the Third Degree attunement and symbol are conveyed and the process of how to go about giving the First Degree attunements is taught and then practiced. Also given are other beneficial practices that help the student absorb the teaching. At the end of this first portion of the training, we usually teach a First Degree class together.

It is then up to the master student to organize and teach a number of First Degree classes for about three to six months, after which time I then teach the process of how to convey the Second Degree attunements. This portion of the training is then completed with a Second Degree class that we teach together. From then on, the master student can begin to teach Second Degree.

It is only after a lengthy period of teaching both First and Second Degree classes that the process for conveying the Third Degree attunement is taught. Part of the contract for Third Degree is that the master student promises not to teach another master student Third Degree for at least three years and to teach at least 20 First Degree classes with a minimum of 12 students (40 classes with five or six students will do) and at least 15 to 20 Second Degree classes. In order to convey the mastership properly, you have to be a well-schooled, very experienced teacher yourself. Beware of so-called masters who have received mastership after only six months experience, not to mention some of the fly-by-night "masters" produced in less than a month.

My advice for potential master students is to fully query your potential teacher. If you are looking for the cheapest (or most famous) master on the block, you are probably not ready for Third Degree. To get the most benefit of Third Degree, find someone who is really willing to take time with you and stretch you to your limit. Find someone who doesn't make you feel small or less than he or she, who honors you and shows you love and respect. Definitely avoid anyone who is attempting to elicit fear in you in any form. In Indian traditions a spiritual teacher is sometimes referred to as "friend in wholesomeness" (*kalyanamitra*). If this is your desire, find your wholesome friend so that you may find peace.

THE HAND POSITIONS OF THE FULL-BODY TREATMENT AND THEIR EFFECT ON THE ENDOCRINE SYSTEM

*T*raditional Reiki emphasizes the importance of first treating the whole body, by utilizing hand positions that cover all the major organs and the key endocrine glands, and only after that completing the treatment on specific trouble spots. The life force needs to be raised throughout the entire body in order to summon the self-healing powers inherent in our physical structure. All of the glands of the endocrine system work together to keep the body in perfect balance. By enhancing and energizing the endocrine glands, much that is out of order will naturally begin to synchronize; once having been mobilized, the innate self-healing power of the body can be brought to bear on the area affected by a specific ailment.

As the body is a whole in which any part or level of structural organization is interrelated and interacts with any other part or level of structural organization, it logically follows that we do have to treat the whole in order to balance and heal the part. Naturally, the opposite is also true: whenever we let just one area of the body draw Reiki, the whole body also benefits indirectly because, no matter where you lay on your hands, the energy is always drawn to where it is most needed.

The spontaneous laying on of hands, wherever we feel drawn to do so, is usually sufficient for the general maintenance of life force energy in your body. However, for treating specific imbalances or ailments, this approach may not provide an energy boost strong enough to make a difference. From this, it logically follows that full-body treatments are required.

In order to understand what is involved, it is helpful to review which areas and systems of the body are covered by the traditional hand positions during a full-body Reiki treatment. By covering the body from head to toe, we inadvertently treat the nervous system, the bones of the skeleton, and the muscles. We also cover many parts of the skin. Furthermore, particular attention is given to the organs, which include the cardiovascular, lymphatic, digestive, urinary, respiratory, and reproductive systems. Throughout the process we also put extra attention on the endocrine system.

Thus, a full-body treatment with Reiki enhances the interplay of the 11 major functional systems of our bodies. For example, through strengthening the circulatory system by letting the heart draw Universal Life Force Energy, we automatically strengthen the respiratory system, because more oxygen-laden blood can be distributed, and more "used" blood filled with carbon dioxide can be delivered for disposal by the lungs. Or, by letting the pancreas draw Reiki, you simultaneously raise the life force energy in your digestive and endocrine systems, because the pancreas happens to be part of both of them.

There are countless similarly important connections. They are far too numerous to mention all of them. However, it might be helpful, for your Reiki practice, to learn more about this miraculous living continuum of the human body—the many interactions among its systems and their mysterious, life-sustaining synergy. Further reading is highly suggested. There are many excellent and beautifully illustrated books available about the workings of the human body. Pick one up at your local library and start investigating on your own. It is helpful to read with your heart as well as with your mind. You can absorb and analyze the factual information, but also allow yourself to be touched by the beauty and incredible complexity of what we call a human body, your very own vehicle for experiencing this dimension. Also know that whatever you learn during your investigation is just a fraction of what is there, because the more factual knowledge you acquire, the more you realize how much more there is that you don't know. Any increase in factual knowledge always automatically increases our ignorance regarding new levels of factual knowledge that are implied by the bits and pieces that have just been uncovered. So it is that we must honor the intuition (the truth) of the moment, in addition to our factual knowledge. It is much like the wisdom of the ancients, which recognizes that we can never really *know* anything, that we can only *experience* it.

Your newly found knowledge will eventually fine-tune the direct sensations and feelings that tend to come up during a treatment and greatly deepen your understanding of Reiki. Clarity and precision will begin to replace vague and cloudy impressions. Of course, feeling directly what is happening in the moment remains the most important factor in your practice. Combined with clear insights into the workings of the human body, the ability to feel will help you to communicate your intuitions and perceptions to yourself and others in a much clearer fashion, which, in turn, will empower you to be of greater assistance.

To help you follow the basic placement of the hands, the following pictures illustrate the main positions. These cover the major organs, as well as the entire endocrine system.

The key thing to remember during a Reiki treatment is to have a relaxed approach. Just loosen up, while you hold your hands in each position on the body. On the other hand, you also don't want to lean too heavily on or press on the area being treated. Always keep one hand on the body as you change positions. In other words, when one position feels complete, first move only one hand slowly and gently to the next, and only then follow with the other hand.

Because Reiki is a form of conscious, noninvasive touch, always keep your awareness in your hands as you very deliberately raise one hand off the body, equally slowly and deliberately move it toward the next position, and then gently place it; use the same procedure as you move the second hand into the same position. Then it is simply a matter of waiting and listening to the signals in your hands—such as tingling, pulsating, or heat—or just an intuitive sense that tells you this position is complete. Then you simply move on.

The answers to questions 20 to 32 provide further suggestions for both self-treatment and the treatment of others. You may want to look them up. At the end of this Appendix, after the pictures that illustrate the most widely accepted treatment protocol for Reiki, you can find additional information on the endocrine system, which serves to explain the effect such treatments may have, especially if done repeatedly.

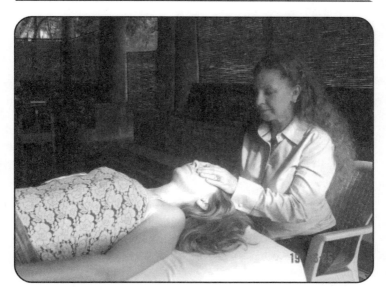

1st Position

For self-treatment: Your options are to either sit or lie down. Gently cup the eyes with the palms of both hands.

When treating another: While standing (or sitting) at the head of the body, place the tips of your fingers along the zygomatic arch (the slightly protruding skeletal structure under the eyes). The thumbs of both hands touch somewhat, covering the space above and between the eyebrows. Make sure that the pointer fingers are placed not so close to the nose that you would press the nostrils. This way you will avoid irritating or even blocking the air passages.

Benefit: This position will contribute to relieving eye strain. It also supports a feeling of general relaxation. In addition, all head positions help sustain the proper function of the pineal and pituitary glands.

2nd Position

For self-treatment: Cup your hands and place them over the temples.

When treating another: While keeping the thumbs on the energy point above and between the eyebrows (Third Eye), move the palms lightly until they are over the temples. The contact should be firm but gentle.

Benefit: This position helps release tension in the band of muscles that fan out from the jaw toward the skullcap, where much stress and tension is habitually stored.

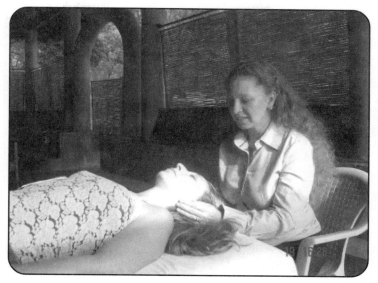

3rd Position

For self-treatment: Cup your hands and place them over the ears.

When treating another: Same as for self. Cup your hands lightly as you change positions, always lifting one hand first, placing it, and then following with the other.

Benefit: When you treat the ears, you automatically give an energy boost to the entire body. Many energy points on the ears are connected to and, thus, reflex to all the major energy channels and various organs in the body (in the same way that key energy points in the hand and feet also reflex). This is the very reason why ear acupuncture and the massage of the energy points along and inside the ears can be so efficient.

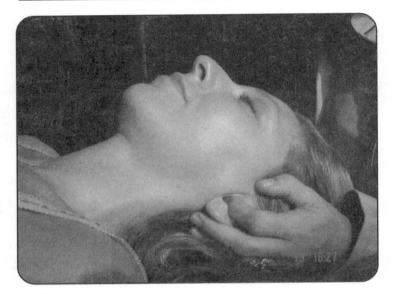

Variation of 3rd Position

For self-treatment: Gently insert both of your pointer fingers simultaneously in the ears, entirely (and carefully) blocking the Eustachian tubes, while you keep the other fingers and the palms of your hands still cupped over the ears.

When treating another: Same as for self. Be subtle and precise about it, so that the other doesn't feel as if his or her space is invaded. Within minutes, this position will provide a deep sense of repose.

Benefit: This position immediately has tremendous benefits, as it brings all the meridians or lines of energy into a balanced steady flow. You will feel immediately refreshed. It sometimes feels as if all the cares of the world have simply fallen away.

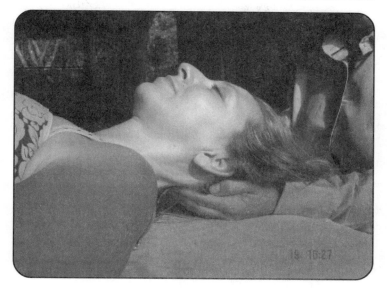

4th Position

For self-treatment: Place both hands in a comfortable way under the occipital lobes (the two protruding bony structures at the lower back part of the skull).

When treating another: Cup your hands under the person's skull, hooking your fingertips feelingly along the edge of the skull, next to the neck. This creates a psychologically nourishing effect, as we totally support the other's head. Once your hands are in place, allow your fingers to completely relax.

Benefit: This position provides a deep letting go of further tension congealed around the head.

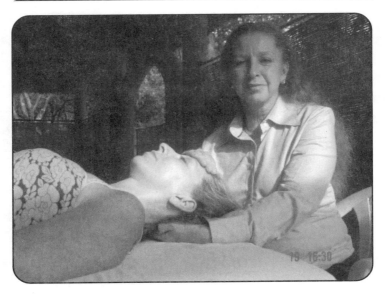

5th Position

For self-treatment: This position is best executed while lying down. Place a pillow to one side of your head and prop your upper arm and elbow on it. Place the same hand on your forehead. Keep the other hand cupped underneath both occipital lobes, as in the previous position.

While treating another: Cup one hand under both occipital lobes and place the other on the forehead as in the position for self-treatment.

Benefit: This has proved to be a good position for relieving headaches, especially those created by excess tension. It also has an overall relaxing effect.

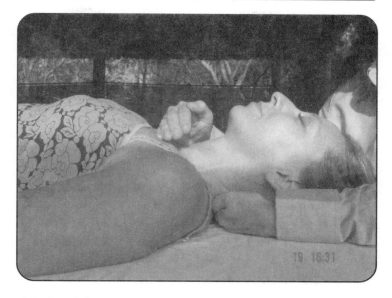

6th Position

For self-treatment: Let the hand that is behind the occipital lobes now slide down until it is placed behind your neck. Hold the other hand suspended over the throat, by supporting it with its outer edge just below your collarbone.

When treating another: Same as for self. Be sure that the edge of the hand rests *lightly* on the collarbone of your client and does not slip carelessly on the windpipe. Really, stay very attentive while treating this position.

Benefit: This position is excellent for sore throats, laryngitis, and similar conditions.

7th Position

For self-treatment: Now begin "stair stepping" the hands down the center line of the body: First, the hand that was over the throat stays there but shifts ever so slightly so that it is slanted forward, toward the lower part of the throat. As a result, the Reiki energy is now more drawn into the thyroid, located in the lower part of the throat. Place the other hand just below the top hand, adjacent to it, so that they are touching (the thumb of the lower hand touches the little finger of the upper hand, which is still hovering over the lower part of the throat). This way, you are also covering the thymus, which is located exactly between the thyroid and the heart.

When treating another: Same as for self.

Benefit: This position particularly acts to strengthen the metabolism of the cells in the entire body and tones circulation. As the thymus gland is closely connected with the immune system, this position also boosts our defenses against invading microorganisms. Contrary to popular belief, the thymus does not stop functioning after puberty but, as recent research shows, continues to play an important role for a well-tuned immune system—even more so when the body's natural defenses have not been compromised by the use of too many drugs and inoculations.

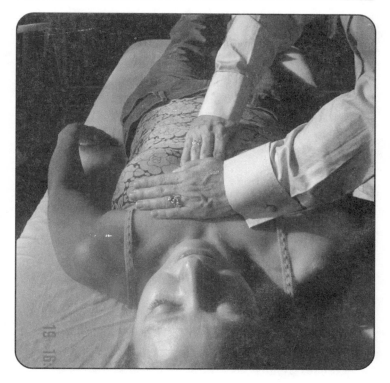

8th Position

For self-treatment: Now cover the heart area with both hands slightly cupped.

When treating another: Same as for self. Note: When treating a woman, you can put one hand between the breasts and the other hand just below them so that your hands form a T.

Benefit: Psychologically, this position is good for taking care of approval issues and the sense of a "lack of love," which most often is a sign of a deeply imbedded resistance to accepting love and/or self-love. As far as its physical effect is concerned, it is also good for treating any cardiac problems.

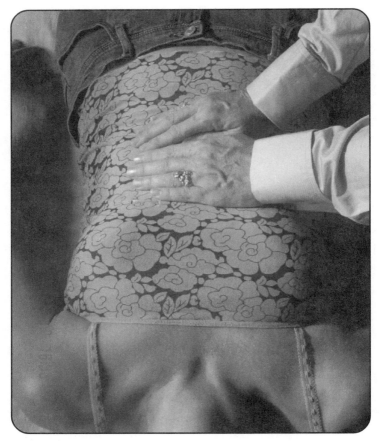

9th Position

In self-treatment: Place both hands over the solar plexus (just below the heart).

When treating another: Same as for self.

Benefit: This position helps to relieve stomachache or nervous tension. On an energetic level, it also facilitates the clearing of any issues, which have to do with trusting one's own inborn power and wisdom.

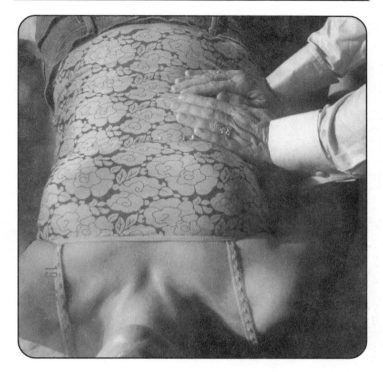

10th Position

For self-treatment: At this point I diverge from the straight line down the body and cover the so-called "four corner" positions, starting with the liver, on the right side of the torso, next to the solar plexus. Put one hand over the lower right lobe of the right rib cage and the other flush with and below that, in order to cover both the liver and the gall bladder.

When treating another: Same as for self.

Benefit: Whenever you are angry for an unnaturally prolonged period of time or feel a lot of anger directed at you, liver/gall bladder is an important position to treat. In addition, this position generally helps to alleviate your system from excess toxins stored throughout the body.

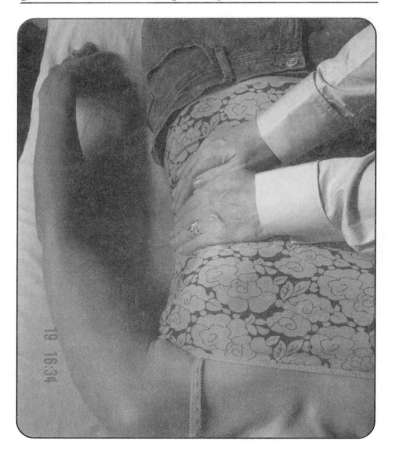

11th Position

For self-treatment: Cover the opposite side of what is described in position 10. In other words, put one hand on the left lower rib cage and the other just below it, and you will be covering the spleen and the pancreas.

When treating another: Same as for self.

Benefit: Especially important in cases of diabetes.

12th Position

For self-treatment: Place each hand on the upper part of the corresponding lung.

When treating another: Same as for self.

Benefit: This is especially important if you are a smoker or live in an environment with air pollution. From this, it logically follows that the 12th position is likewise helpful in the case of asthma.

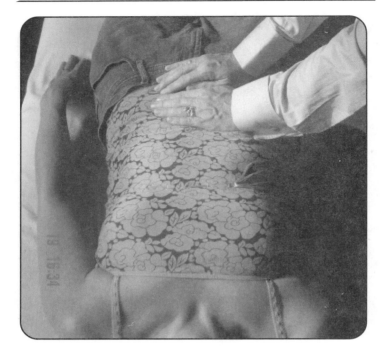

13th Position

For self-treatment: Now move the hands back to the center line of the body; place one hand directly over the navel and the other right below it.

When treating another: Same as for self.

Benefit: Psychologically, this position is important in order to help you get in touch with unacknowledged and suppressed feelings. Note that men will usually draw a lot of energy in this position due to their conditioned suppression of feelings. Treating this area will help bring up "gut" feelings that need to be felt. This area, as well as the heart, is helpful for treating depression (which is not a feeling, but a suppression of feelings). Physically, it is indicated for any digestive disorders and pathological conditions in the bowels.

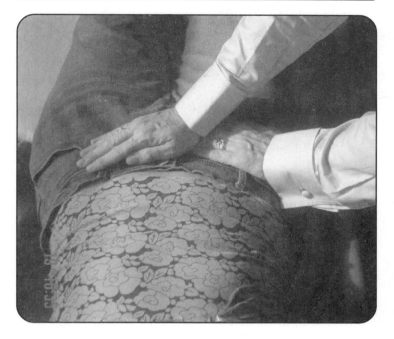

14th Position (Women)

For self-treatment: Place palms in a V-shape, pointed inwards toward each other, so that the tips of the fingers are touching and the hands are placed along the upper edge of the pubic *ramus*, the bone above the pubic area. This will ensure that both uterus and ovaries are covered.

When treating another: With your hands, create a crescent moon shape so that they follow the lower curve of the abdomen and are lined up against the pubic ramus.

Benefit: This will help prevent ovarian cysts as well as uterine fibroids later in life. If you treat this area repeatedly, over a longer period of time, the 14th position can also balance any disharmony regarding sexual issues that you might have, which are stored in the memory bank of the cells in this area.

14th Position (Men)

For self-treatment: Cup your hands over your genitals.

When treating another: You can either treat by letting your hands hover above the genitals of your client or, preferably, by laying the hands over the *inguinal nodes*, the small glands which are located between the uppermost part of the thighs and the base of the genitals (where the leg and the torso attach). It is easiest to point the palms toward each other, yet apart over both inguinal nodes on either side of the body.

Benefit: This position will help preclude prostrate problems in later years. It will also contribute to a strong and healthy male sexuality and help dissolve any unbalanced fixations regarding the aggressive display of sexual prowess at all times, which is actually a sign of an unacknowledged fear of weakness.

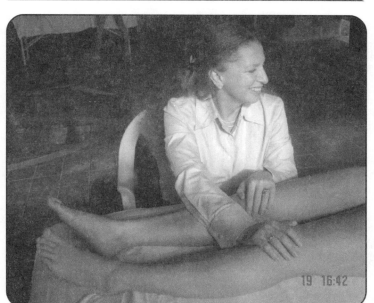

15th Position

For self-treatment: If you have been lying down, at this point you will need to sit up. Cup each hand over your knees. (This can also be done while sitting at a desk or in a bus.)

When treating another: Cup your hands over both knees of your client simultaneously, as for self. If you are using a massage table, you can usually sit comfortably at this point to treat the other, while he or she keeps in the supine position.

Benefit: This is an important position for all of us, living in today's stressful world. According to body psychology, the knees represent fear of change (including fear of both physical death, as well death of the ego). In this day and age, we are all undergoing change at such a tremendous rate that the knees can always use a little extra attention.

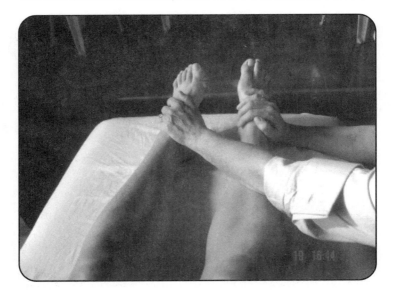

16th Position

For self-treatment: Treat the tops of the feet by placing one hand over the top of each foot.

When treating another: Same as for self.

Benefit: Feet have energy points for the entire body, as they are the place of origin and end points for many energy pathways or meridians, according to many different systems of energy medicine. This is why reflexology and foot massage are a part of folk medicine in different cultures around the world.

17th Position

For self-treatment: Place one hand fully over the bottom of each foot.

When treating another: Same as for self.

Benefit: Treating your feet is a short form of treating the entire body. It also supports your sense of feeling grounded in your own direct inner and outer experience, which can support you in taking charge of your own life.

18th Position

For self-treatment: Place your hands on top of your shoulders touching the fingertips together so that they cover the top part of the spine over the seventh cervical vertebra. For some, it is easier to execute this position by crisscrossing their arms.

When treating another: Make a crescent moon shape with your hands, by touching the tips of the fingers of one hand to the heel of the other hand and tilting one so that you create a slight V-shape from the point where both hands touch at the nape of the neck.

Benefit: This position is especially important for people who tend to literally carry "the weight of the world" on their shoulders. This is especially the case for women, who are more often prone to taking on supporting roles. If unbalanced, habitually assuming the role of the caretaker will create lots of tension and pain, or tight knots in the muscles, which, in turn, will frequently trigger migraine headaches.

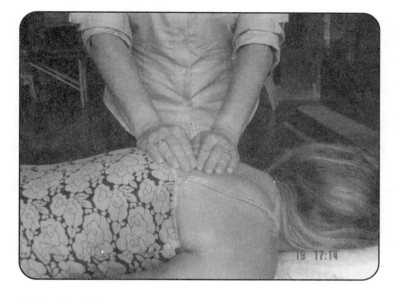

19th Position

For self-treatment: Not possible.

When treating another: Place both hands over the back of the heart.

Benefit: The heart can always use extra treatment on the back as well. A lot of excess tension is often stored in the *spinalis* muscles in this area. Treating the back of the heart is a good preventive measure against back problems caused by emotional trauma.

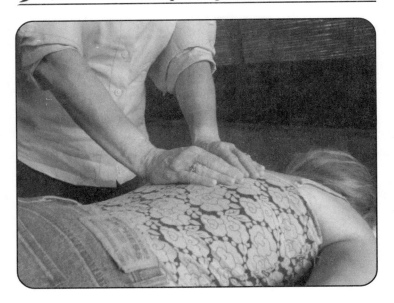

20th Position

For self-treatment: Generally not possible.

When treating another: Place both hands over the back of the solar plexus.

Benefit: Tension in this area often is connected with control issues. Long treatments over the back of the solar plexus help in greater relaxation and in regaining trust in one's own resources.

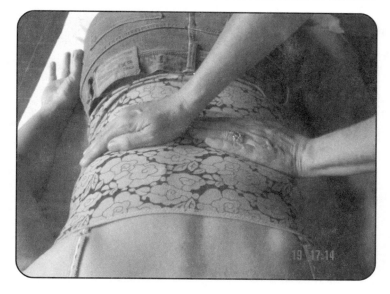

21st Position

For self-treatment: Place both hands over the kidney/ adrenal area. You can easily find the kidneys by placing both hands approximately one hand-width above the small of the waist on both sides. The adrenal glands are attached to the kidneys, positioned right above them.

When treating another: Same as for self. Place one hand over each kidney, located one hand-width above the small of the waist (hands are in line with one another across the person's back).

Benefit: Treatment is especially indicated when we are under a lot of stress. The adrenal glands also support the function of the kidneys, bones, bone marrow, and spine. Thus, treating this position supports the function of all of the previous organs. (Note: the drug cortisone destroys the adrenal glands, causing anemia and bone weakening!)

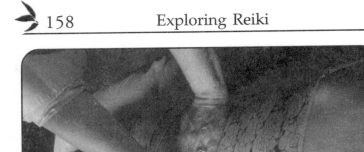

22nd Position

For self-treatment: Place both hands at the small of the waist.

When treating another: Place your hands across the waist, in line with one another (tips of the fingers of one hand touching the heel of the other).

Benefit: Helps to give relief to lower back problems and helps release any suppressed emotion stored in the area.

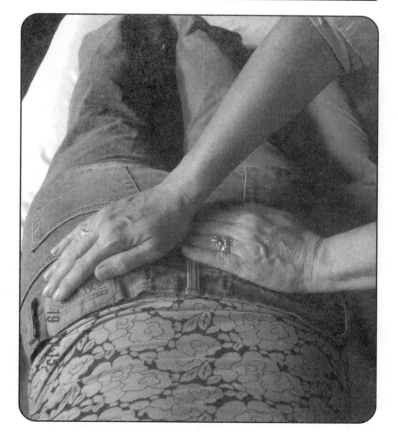

23rd Position

For self-treatment: Place hands along the *sacro-iliac* crest.

When treating another: Place hands across the lower back, in line with one another, at the level of the sacrum. Hands should create a slight V or crescent moon shape to go with the slight curve at the beginning of the *gluteus* muscles of the buttocks.

Benefit: This helps relieve stress in the lower spine, around the sacrum.

24th Position

For self-treatment: Not possible.

When treating another: To complete a treatment and balance the energies of the spine, let one hand hover an inch or two above the sacrum and feel where the energy seems to draw the most. Then place one hand on that very spot on the sacrum. Let the other hand then hover above the area of the seventh cervical vertebra (C7) at the base of the neck until you get a sense where the energy seems strongest. Place the other hand there. Listen into both hands until you feel equal heat, vibration, tingling, pulsation, or just an intuition that the energies in both places are in perfect balance. Then slowly and very gradually, without disturbing the energy field of the healee, withdraw the hands from the body. Then make a V with the fingers of one hand and, placing the two sides of the V on either side of the spine, on the C7 vertebra, draw the fingers briskly down the back several times to stimulate the circulation and wake the person up. This can be done very lightly, if the person has dozed off in the course of the treatment.

Benefit: This position balances the flow of energies in the entire spine, and because the spine is the central axis of our body, it has an overall psychophysical balancing effect.

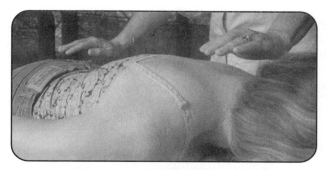

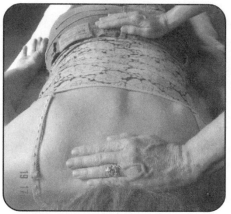

Reiki always acts in the same manner: it raises the life force energy and calms the mind. In other words, it simultaneously hones your energy *and* creates balance. The more the whole body is suffused with it, the higher and more balanced will its vibratory frequency become; that is, it becomes less susceptible to disharmony, degeneration, and atrophy. A key to dispersing Reiki throughout the entire body is to place special emphasis on the endocrine system.

Together with the interlocking nervous system, we could call the endocrine system the main regulator of the body. It consists of several glands of internal secretion that yield the hormones which govern our growth from childhood to adulthood and control our sexual development. It is also closely connected to, and interacts with, the immune system, which protects us against disease. These systems and the hormones they produce direct virtually every bodily function, from breathing, to digestion, to reproduction, to fending off disease. They enable the body to deal with heat, cold, stress, and starvation and help it to protect itself against dehydration, infection, trauma, and bleeding. They also control the volume of the body fluids and their chemical composition and balance.

The endocrine, or ductless, glands are: the hypothalamus, the pineal gland, the pituitary gland, the thyroid and parathyroid glands, the thymus, the adrenal cortex and medulla, the pancreas, the ovaries (in women), and the testes (in men). They produce most of the hormones that control a multitude of functions and rhythms of the body. However, several other organs also secrete hormones. The stomach, liver, intestines, kidneys, and heart all contain clusters of cells which emit hormones into the bloodstream, and thus become part of the endocrine system (although they themselves are not endocrine glands, in the strictest sense of the word).

It would go beyond the scope of this short essay to fully describe the entire workings of the endocrine system. Two examples will suffice to illustrate the case in point. They may give you a better idea of its importance and motivate you to learn more about it and also to direct more Reiki to the endocrine glands.

Since ancient times, the pineal gland was believed to be important, although in most historical periods—and especially in western culture—little was known about this tiny structure in the shape of a pine cone (hence its name). To the French philosopher and mathematician René Descartes, the pineal gland was the mysterious place where "mind and body meet." Today, our knowledge is more specific. We now realize that, in one sense, the pineal gland serves as an internal clock, regulating the circadian rhythms of the body—it makes sure that we stay attuned to daily and seasonal changes. It enables us to live in synchronicity with nature by regulating the body's wake/sleep cycle in accordance with the earth's cycle of day and night.

However, regulating the body's wake/sleep cycle is just one of the many tasks taken up by the pineal gland. Its even more crucial function, according to recent research, is akin to a lifelong internal timer. In this capacity, the pineal gland performs the task of the body's aging clock, which controls the aging process by releasing the hormone melatonin, which then transmits information to other systems in the body telling them how and when to age. In other words, our physical bodies grow up, mature, and degenerate because the melatonin level in the pineal gland instructs them to. The adult peak level for melatonin is at around age 20, but by age 60 we have only half of the melatonin available with further dramatic slips that continue and, of course, accelerate the process of degeneration even further into what we usually call "old age."

The question then is, does this new found knowledge about the function of the pineal gland give us a clue about a potential slowing down of the aging process? It very well may. Some even go so far as to suggest that, by treating the body with hormonal supplements, we are actually able not only to stop but to reverse the aging process. In the context of Reiki, another question then arises, if we can indeed reset the aging clock in the pineal gland by supplementing the body with melatonin, would regular Reiki treatments on this very gland achieve the same goal of maintaining life in a strong and healthy body—even in old age—so that you would eventually die without being subjected to the typical ailments of degeneration? Historical accounts from Taoist and Tantric masters and adepts who have channeled and applied Universal Life Force Energy in their practice strongly suggest this as a fact.

However, at this point, we have to acknowledge how truly groundbreaking Mrs. Takata's focus on the endocrine system really was during her lifetime, because most of the information on the endocrine system available now had not yet come out in 1980, when she passed away. Actually, until the late 70s, most researchers still believed that every gland and every organ system performed solo, wholly independent of other glands and organ systems. It was proved later that the glands of the endocrine system are in constant contact and interaction with the cells of the immune system. Still later, it was found that there must be some governing agency in the body that was designed to coordinate the exchange of information to carry out the task of executing all of these functions.

The pineal gland is this governing agency. As long as it produces sufficient amounts of melatonin, our immune system will remain vigorous and we will continue to be endowed with high levels of lymphocytes (which create antibodies and suppress unwanted invaders). The level of the hormones particular to the thyroid can then also remain high to provide for a corresponding level of energy. It is also very likely that health will be maintained into the very last days of our life and that age-related cancer will not occur, which is why regular Reiki on the pineal gland will promote much more than simple longevity. It will also greatly enhance the quality of life.

The most important quality of Reiki is that it releases tension and stress. Reiki was designed to calm the mind and raise the life force energy. In this way, it exerts a strong healing influence on the immune system and may prevent much stress-induced illness.

Stress causes a great deal of damage to the immune system. There are many studies available on the subject that prove, beyond any doubt, that stress-induced illness is indeed happening and that stress is at least a contributing factor in many diseases—and very often actually triggers it. Stress takes many forms in a human being, for example: conflicts at home, work related anxieties, sleep deprivation, the typical modern-day over-stimulation of the senses combined with a simultaneous lack of physical exercise, taking care of chronically ill family members, and so forth. Immune suppression and stress can therefore be regarded as synonymous.

In other words, the more stress there is in your life and the more you *identify* with this stress by perceiving yourself as its victim, the more suppressed your immune system will become and the more you are likely to suffer from stress-induced illness—particularly if your personal response to outside stress is to create even more inner strife and stress.

Basically, stress awakens the flight-or-fight response. It stimulates the sympathetic nervous system and suppresses the parasympathetic nervous system, which is responsible for bodily functions in times of rest, relaxation, meditation, and deep sleep. It shouldn't come as a surprise to us that the immune system functions better when the parasympathetic nervous system kicks in and takes over. On the other hand, when the body is preparing to fight or flee, dealing with an invading microorganism is definitely not its top priority.

The secretion of stress-induced adrenal gland hormones then inhibit white blood cell function and lower the production of lymphocytes. Continued subjection to external and reactive internal stress may even cause the thymus gland to shrink (the thymus gland being the master gland of the immune system). A significant reduction in immune system activity is both the immediate and long-term result. The message is clear and simple: stress really does damage immune function.

Regular Reiki on all the glands of the endocrine system, particularly on the area of the thymus gland will counteract this trend and eventually lead to an alteration in the neurotransmitters in your brain, because you will open gradually to more positive thoughts, such as love, compassion, peace, personal courage, commitment, and self-actualization.

As we all know from our own experience, negative thoughts make us feel down (in other words, they suppress the immune system). Positive thoughts, on the other hand, when palpably felt, stimulate the immune system. More studies on the effect of positive thoughts on the neurotransmitters in our brain are coming out every year, changing the focus of research from disease-producing mechanisms to health-engendering mechanisms (which in itself is a very healthy change).

Through actively supporting neuro-immune modulation in the course of a treatment or self-treatment (by strengthening the interaction between the endocrine and immune systems of the body and their links to the brain), Reiki is quickly becoming a gentle form of mind/body medicine. Regular application of Universal Life Force Energy will have a spill-over effect on pretty much every area of your life.

Provided you do Reiki more than just once in a while, it is very likely that the four primary areas of expression will be affected by the regular application of Universal Life Force Energy. As a result, in your daily existence, you will find a new, mutually enhancing, and nurturing balance. You will intuitively know how long it is appropriate to work, when you need to play, when and where it is appropriate to open yourself to love, and when and how to express your deep faith in Self.

WHY REIKI?

*N*aturopathy suggests that there is really only one healing power in existence, and that is Nature Herself. In Reiki, we call this healing power Universal Life Force Energy, which includes, but goes far beyond, the ordinary inherent restorative power of the body to battle and vanquish disease. As an added benefit it touches upon and includes the potential for complete self-realization in moment-to-moment awareness. Because in Reiki we directly work with energy, Reiki itself is considered a form of energy medicine.

As in other forms of natural healing, Reiki also stresses the importance of health maintenance and disease prevention, which is a much cheaper and more effective approach to well-being than the common focus on curing manifest diseases. Toward the end of his life, even Louis Pasteur, the father of the allopathic "war on germs," conceded as much. Throughout his professional life, Pasteur had fought for the acceptance of his theory that each disease is produced by a different infectious microorganism. On the grounds of this view, he had battled fellow French scientist Claude Bernard, who held forth that the *susceptibility* of an individual to these infectious microorganisms was actually more important than the microorganisms themselves. Although Pasteur eventually convinced pretty much everyone of the correctness of his views, he himself was forthright enough to admit that he had been wrong, because shortly before his death he himself stated: "Bernard was right. The pathogen is nothing. The terrain is everything." Which means that even Pasteur finally came to see that the state of a person's internal environment contributes much more to their tendency to manifest a disease than the infecting organisms or pathogens themselves.

Although antibiotics are extremely helpful in cases of serious infections and life-threatening diseases, the general obsession with the killing of invading microorganisms (rather than strengthening and supporting the immune system through maintaining good health and psychophysical balance) automatically leads to many instances of improper usage. The misuse of these powerful antibiotic agents, such as prescribing them thoughtlessly for a common cold or flu, has become rampant in many countries in the world. Through the misuse that has occured over the past 40 to 50 years, we are in danger of losing their curative powers, because more and more microorganisms are becoming resistant to antibiotics. According to many experts we are already living in the "post-antibiotic era," in which numerous infectious diseases are once again almost as incurable as they were in the "pre-antibiotic era."

This is why the nature cure or Reiki approach to maintaining good health are crucial not only to individual well-being but to a healthier healthcare system in general. The need for a healthier approach to healthcare is precisely why many medical doctors on the cutting edge are looking for a more holistic paradigm. Although still in the minority, their numbers are increasing steadily. With insurance companies, in the framework of so-called "managed care," now dictating the types of treatments physicians can use, doctors are becoming painfully aware of the disruptive and outright destructive ways in which the present-day healthcare industry is destroying actual healthcare.

Indeed, much is afoul with the still predominant paradigm which views good health only as a physical state that reflects the absence of any manifest disease. We basically can no longer afford an approach which is about to bankrupt us both physically and fiscally. We have no other choice but to support techniques and therapies that will teach us how to stay well. The following figures speak for themselves:

According to the *American Journal of Health Promotion*, we spent $1 Trillion ($1,000,000,000,000!) on the treatment of diseases in the United States in 1994, and the expenditures for so-called "healthcare" have skyrocketed by a whopping 300 percent in the last 15 years alone. Disease is obviously a very lucrative business! At present, the treatment of diseases consumes more than 15 percent of the gross national product of this country and continues to rise at twice the rate of inflation (whereas in 1930 it only consumed 1.9 percent)!

Obviously, something went terribly wrong, because not only do Americans spend more money than ever on the treatment of disease, they are, on the average, also less healthy than they were when they spent only 10 percent of what they are spending now! What happened?

The reasons are many, but they can pretty much be summarized in two factors: In the 1930s, big money interests started to push for legislation which severely restricted (and, to a larger extent today, continues to restrict and even terrorize) complementary approaches to healthcare. At the same time, through different foundations under the guise of charity, the drug industry began to pour big dollars into medical schools, gradually seeing to it that curriculums were changed in a way that would profit them down the road. In short, disease began to have commercial value, and health went down the tubes.

In the 60s and 70s, the government stepped in and made the situation even worse. Federal and state subsidies inflated the number of graduating medical doctors, doubling the rate between 1965 and 1980 so that, in 1992, there were 245 doctors per 100,000 Americans, whereas in 1970 the ratio had been 151 doctors per 100,000 Americans—a staggering increase of 62 percent! Furthermore, most of the new doctors are not general practitioners, but specialists who tend to prescribe and utilize the most expensive procedures. This might at first seem to be a tribute to modern healthcare. Wouldn't the fact that there are more specialists at hand and ready to help imply that Americans are medically better cared for than ever before?

Not so, concludes a study conducted in the late 80s which found that a geographical area with 4.5 surgeons per 10,000 population had 940 operations whereas an area with 2.5 surgeons for the same amount of people experienced only 590 operations in the same stretch of time. To put it bluntly: If you double the amount of surgeons, you end up with double the amount of surgeries! The question then is: are they all necessary?

You bet they aren't, says another study, published in the *Journal of the American Medical Association*, on 168 patients who were either scheduled or counseled to undergo coronary artery bypass surgery. The study found the proposed surgery in 80 percent of the cases either unnecessary or inappropriate. In other words, fewer than 34 of 168 patients set for surgery really needed surgery!

Many things are wrong with our view of the treatment of disease and with the healthcare industry, which is in the business of making money from diseases (not from health and well-being), it is no wonder that we no longer hear much reference to healing as an art. The way the game is set up right now, it is virtually impossible to shift the interest of the "health" care industry to health, because too much money is made from disease. This doesn't imply a sinister conspiracy by individual healthcare practitioners such as doctors and nurses. Most try their best, according to their training and the information that is available to them. Quite a few would be shocked if they knew that the costs of preventable diseases and deaths related to prescription drugs amounted to $77 billion in the early 90s and are most likely considerably higher now!

Despite the trillion dollars spent on the treatment of disease (or is it *because* that much money was spent?), almost half of all working Americans are in ill health or suffer from a chronic disease (such as arthritis, high blood pressure, diabetes, and so forth). Please take note that this figure only takes into account people in their prime, who are part of the work force. The numbers for the elderly are far worse, virtually all of whom are afflicted by one or more chronic and/or degenerative conditions!

All of this data, of which there is much more on iatrogenic (physician-caused) disease, clearly suggest that a change in outlook is called for. A shift in focus is needed from treating disease to maintaining health. Because of its openness and versatility, as well as its emphasis on prevention, Reiki is an integral part of the newly emerging care for the whole person. According to this new paradigm, health is seen as a state of optimal physical, mental, emotional, and spiritual well-being—or, to use another common phrase, as total wellness. Total wellness is also both the nature and the aim of Universal Life Force Energy.

The pending shift in the healthcare paradigm, by the way, does not mean that we have to discard anything which was gained over many years or even generations of dedicated medical research. There will always be a place for state-of-the-art modern allopathic forms of treatment, simply because there are countless instances when they are a real blessing and save lives, as in trauma surgery, for example.

Nowhere in this book or in this short essay is it inferred that Reiki should *replace* other forms of medical intervention. Reiki is, in itself, a complete form of energy medicine, but it is not necessarily a cure-all, in the same way that no other form of medicine is. Each discipline offers its own wonderful tools to promote the healing process. When skillfully combined, different forms of medicine can help heal a myriad of conditions. The greatest benefit of any healing art is in strengthening the mind/body continuum to better withstand disease.

In countries such as India or China, which still have a living tradition of age-old disease prevention and holistic healthcare such as Ayurveda or Acupuncture, many allopaths are beginning to see the light and adopt some of the ancient tried and true practices. They are well advised to keep their old systems in place and only supplement them with modern western allopathy, in the areas where the old system does not provide for the same advanced level of care. The figures and trends discussed previously clearly demonstrate the need for caution concerning any wholesale dismissal of long proven, age-old healing arts with a several thousand year success rate. The ongoing sneaky attempt—and partial success—by multinational pharmaceutical companies to patent common ancient Ayurvedic remedies, such as neem and turmeric (most often to keep them *out* of circulation), should act as a major wake up call to people everywhere who value freedom of choice in caring for their own bodies.

THE REIKI DECLARATION OF INDEPENDENCE

*T*he practice of Reiki amounts to a powerful personal Declaration of Independence from the crutches and clutches of the typical passive consumer approach to well-being still predominant in this country and throughout the Westernized world. With Reiki, you are, in effect, boldly stating that you are (or at least have direct access to) the very energy that the entire cosmos is made of and that, furthermore, this energy will henceforth be the main source of your health and happiness.

This implies that you find certain truths self-evident, first and foremost among which is the insight that, in order to be well, you have to be in charge of all matters regarding your own physical, psychological, and spiritual well-being. You cease to delegate this power to someone else. Although you will remain perfectly open and available to listen to pertinent advice, you reserve the right to act on *any* outside information, according to your own deliberations (and after getting at least a second or even third opinion from any source of your own choice). You decide. You don't let so-called specialists decide for you.

In other words, you empower yourself to stand up for the truth that you, like all women and men everywhere throughout the whole world, are created equal by the God Force and that you, therefore, have certain unalienable rights, such as the right to life, liberty, and the *pursuit* of your own happiness.

You fully understand that Natural Law cannot grant you the right to happiness, for the simple reason that such a "right" would take away your power. Anyone who claims to give you the right to something beyond the basic rights such as life, liberty, and the pursuit of happiness, in effect, is attempting to grant you a privilege. The problem with privileges (which are similar to inferior civil rights as compared to natural, *unalienable* rights) is that they can be revoked by the very people who appoint themselves to grant them. A right based on Natural Law, on the other hand, is not as shaky as a mere privilege. It can never be taken away from you, because it is your birthright as a free human being.

The right to the pursuit of your own happiness includes the right to choose how you want to take care of your own health. In other words, you have the right to choose the method of treatment you prefer. If there is any outside interference in this process, then your natural right to the pursuit of your own happiness has been usurped and taken away from you. Furthermore, with the practice of Reiki, you make a bold statement that you are well equipped to maintain your own health.

You acknowledge that the body is not a machine separate from all other bodies and all of creation, but that it partakes in the same energies that everything is fundamentally made of. You know that in order to heal the body you will have to address the wholeness that you are, or if you are working as a healthcare professional, that you will always have to address the whole patient (client). You are aware that your focus has to shift from the elimination of disease to achieving and maintaining good health. As a healthcare practitioner, you are not so much preoccupied with treating symptoms but rather graduate to the higher level of treating the underlying physical, emotional, socio-economic, and spiritual causes. You no longer buy into the lie that you have to be emotinally shut down and removed (like a psychotherapist or doctor who believes that he has to protect himself from his patient's feelings) in order to heal yourself and others; instead, you know that a little bit of empathy goes a long way and that directly feeling your own and/or another's pain (which helps release it and allow it to flow through) is actually the first step to removing the causes of this very same pain. In other words, you stop focusing solely on objective information (charts, statistics, test results, book knowledge) to the exclusion of all other sources of information; and in addition, you take into account how you yourself or your patient (client) are feeling.

Treating yourself and others with Universal Life Force Energy, you do not become dogmatic in any way. In a spirit of eclecticism, you may draw from a number of healing arts to create balance in your body/mind, or in that of your client/patient. By fostering your own inner wisdom, you trust your intuition to make your own decisions regarding your health.

The most important effects of Reiki are in prevention and perhaps in its ability to change your outlook and attitude from one of dependency and uninformed consumerism to a spirit of sovereignty and self-reliance. If you treat yourself with Universal Life Force Energy, in full-body sessions on a regular basis, profound changes are bound to happen. In all likelihood, you will become what you essentially always are, but may not notice: a free, sane, and healthy individual, not to be conned any more (if you ever were) to remain the passive and uninformed consumer who takes everything at face value and refrains from challenging anyone who has usurped the authority that is actually yours. Quite the contrary, you take matters regarding your health into your own hands, with your life becoming much the better for it.

Such profound changes usually don't occur overnight. They unfold gradually, and Reiki will remain your dependable companion until they are complete.

PAULA'S REIKI LINEAGE

Dr. Mikao Usui
↓
Dr. Chujiro Hayashi
↓
Hawayo Takata
↓
Barbara Weber Ray
↓
Maureen O'Toole
(who was trained by both
Mrs. Takata and Barbara Ray)
↓
Kate Nani
↓
Dr. Laxmi Paula Horan

INDEX

ABOUT THE AUTHOR

LAXMI PAULA HORAN is a psychologist, Reiki master, author, and seminar leader whose warmth and inspirational teaching help motivate her students to manifest the richness inherent in their lives. In the 1990s, she spent several years with her Indian Jnana Yoga Master, Shri H.W.L. Poonjaji, a self-realized being and student of the famous Shri Ramana Maharshi of Tiruvanamalai. Poonjaji passed away in 1997. Inspired by him, she shifted her focus from self-improvement to self-inquiry, or *vichar*, which brings awareness into the present moment. Since 1998, she has continued this work within the Tibetan Vajrayana tradition.

Born in America, she lived her childhood years in Italy and Germany. She completed her undergraduate studies with a B.A. in Sociology and English Literature in Britain, and then passed both her M.A. (focusing on dance therapy) and her Ph.D. in Psychology in San Diego, California.

Paula has been a guest on radio and TV shows in the United States, Europe, and India. Her first book, *Empowerment Through Reiki*, has been translated into 15 languages. It was followed by *Abundance Through Reiki*, which was released in 1995. Since then *Core Empowerment*, *The Ultimate Reiki Touch*, *The 9 Principles of Self-Healing*, and *The Oxygen Wave* have been added to the list.

Paula welcomes the questions and feedback of her readers. She strives to answer every letter personally, although it may take a few months for the answer to reach its destination, due to her periodic travels. Please e-mail all inquiries regarding this book, requests for seminar schedules, or your interest in organizing a seminar to sunaga09@yahoo.com. To be informed about Dr. Horan's worldwide activities go to *www.paulahoran.com*, where several other related sites can be reached by direct link.